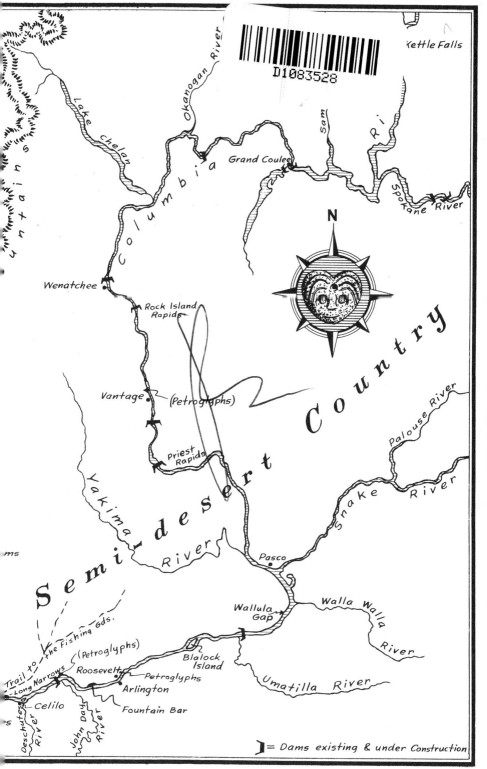

1200

Kettle Falls

Mountains

Lake Chelan

Okanogan River

Columbia

Grand Coulee

Sam

Ri

Spokane River

N

Wenatchee

Rock Island Rapids

Vantage ─ (Petroglyphs)

Semidesert Country

Palouse River

Priest Rapids

Yakima River

Snake River

Pasco

Wallula Gap

Walla Walla River

Trail to the Fishing Gds.

(Petroglyphs)

Long Narrows

Roosevelt

Blalock Island

Petroglyphs

Umatilla River

Celilo

Arlington

Fountain Bar

Deschutes River

John Day River

⟩ = Dams existing & under Construction

Stone Age

on the Columbia River

By

EMORY STRONG

BINFORDS & MORT, *Publishers*

Portland · Oregon · 97242

Stone Age on the Columbia

Printed in the United States of America
Second Edition—Second Printing 1967

FOREWORD

"THIS is certainly a fertil and handsom valley, at this time crouded with Indians" wrote Lewis and Clark of the lower Columbia River valley on their historic journey to the West.

But this was before the white invasion; thirty years later the tribes were practically extinct. John K. Townsend, naturalist with the Wyeth expedition, said in 1835 "Probably there does not now exist one, where, five years ago, there were a hundred Indians; and in sailing up the river, from the cape to the Cascades, the only evidence of the existence of the Indian, is an occasional miserable wigwam, with a few wretched, half starved occupants. In some other places they are rather more numerous; but the thoughtful observer cannot avoid perceiving that in a very few years the race must, in the nature of things, become extinct; and the time is not far distant when the trinkets and toys of this people will be picked up by the curious, and valued as mementos of a nation passed away forever from the face of the earth." But for thousands of years the valley had been a homeland for a large population and their culture reflected the abundance of nature engendered by the mild climate and the River of Life, the Columbia, which teemed with migrating fish for several months each year.

Generations of inhabitants enriched the great valley with relics, and searching for those mementos of the past is a fascinating and absorbing hobby. These ancient people left no written history, but the record is there, hidden deep in the mounds of refuse accumulated on their village sites, and in their burial grounds. From the artifacts and the structure and nature of the deposits it is possible to reconstruct the stone age culture. This story is an open book to those who will learn the language. But the Columbia valley, unlike many other areas in the United

1

States, is almost unexplored, scientifically speaking. Some work has been done, racing the rising waters behind monumental dams; but this work has been mostly in the quite modern sites. Now it is too late, most of the ancient past is buried beneath the raised waters and the tailings of amateur diggers.

What has been preserved is largely in the collections of amateurs and it is from them that the story must be reconstructed. Mr. Thomas C. Colt, Jr., while director of the Portland Art Museum, said, "While the scientific mind may say that these self-dubbed amateurs have seriously disturbed sites where scientific evidence might have been obtained—true no doubt in many instances—nevertheless the vagaries of the river in flood and drought, time and erosion, not to mention the technological improvements of the white man himself, have already confused the sites and scattered or destroyed much evidence. That what we have preserved, is due in large part to those to whom I bow." There is much information in a collection well preserved, catalogued, and displayed. Would that the amateur were as diligent in keeping records as he is in his enthusiasm for the search, that his camera and notebook would ever accompany the shovel and screen! A relic is but an inanimate thing without the record, valueless except as a curiosity.

In this story of the Columbia and its prehistory I make no claim for originality; it is not a treatise on any research into the past, for I am relic hunter only—one of the fast-growing group who are pleased to call themselves "amateur archaeologists." The ethnological material herein I have gleaned from various authors; but all errors are my own. In the back pages is a list of authors and their works. While this does not include all from whom information was extracted, it does present a fairly comprehensive coverage of the history and prehistory of the river, and all are well worth reading. The authors cited throughout the book are listed in the bibliography. There are frequent references to Lewis and Clark. These explorers were not only remarkably keen observers and able recorders, but had the opportunity of association with the Indians before their culture was substantially altered by white influence. About the mouth of the Columbia this influence was already apparent, by 1806, but had not yet reached far upstream. At Umatilla, Lt. Clark, unobserved, shot a crane in flight near an Indian village, and upon entering the camp found the natives in a panic. They had never heard a gun or seen a white man. "They said we came from the clouds &c. &c. and were not men &c. &c." They refused to be placated until they saw Sacajawea. In their writings, Lewis and Clark were completely without emotion; their records are not influenced by contempt and prejudice, as are those of later arrivals whose mission was to exploit.

All photographs in this book were taken by the author unless otherwise credited, and all artifacts are prehistoric —products of the stone age. Excepted are those used in the chapter on trade goods. All are from the Columbia River. Some of the pictures have appeared previously in *Screenings*, the monthly publication of the Oregon Archaeological Society. Beneath each picture or in the text is the name of the collector who owns the artifact, and without whose help this work could not have been written. Where ownership is not shown the piece is from the author's collection. If this book serves any useful purpose it is but small compensation for the many happy hours this writer has spent along the shores of the Columbia, that grandest of all rivers, and the enjoyment of association with the many pleasant personalities of similar interests, both professional and amateur.

CONTENTS

PART I
THE SETTING

THE COLUMBIA RIVER

The Columbia is one of the great rivers of the world, with a drainage area of 259,000 square miles and a length of 1,200 miles. The flow fluctuates widely, rising in the spring when the snows melt and dropping during the fall and winter. In flood it is an awesome sight, tearing at its banks as though angry with its confines, and casting up sand banks and building flood plains in the lowlands. The maximum recorded flow was 125,000,000 cubic feet per second during the flood of 1894, and the lowest was 35,000 in 1937, both measured at The Dalles, Oregon. Discharging more water than any river in the United States except the Mississippi, it has a fall of 1,288 feet from the Canadian border to the sea, making it one of the world's greatest sources of power, a considerable portion of which has already been harnessed.

The Cascade Mountains divide the Columbia River Valley into two distinct areas. To the west, in prehistoric times, from Alaska to California, a soft green blanket two-hundred-feet thick smothered life from the land; only in rents torn through by the rivers were the resident natives able to exist. The river furnished food and means of transportation; its floods maintained the prairies and marshes from which they gathered roots and game. They lived in large permanent villages, had many cedar canoes, and were happy and prosperous. From the forest they took firewood and cedar for their woodwork. Other than this, it was a region held in awe and some terror. Few places on earth are more desolate of life than a western rain forest; no sunlight can penetrate the canopy to sus-

7

tain life, and one can walk a whole day and see no living creature except perhaps a wren or two.

Eastward of the Cascades is a dry region of sparse vegetation interlaced with fertile valleys and flat semi-arid deserts which the Columbia, by power and irrigation, is today transforming into a rich farming country. But in prehistoric times the natives here were rovers, traveling by foot or perhaps by canoe from camas prairie to fishing grounds to berry fields; the horse did not come until about 1720. Houses were semi-subterranean or were made of rush mats. Winters were spent on small streams and rivers, such as the Yakima and Klickitat.

Man may have arrived on the Columbia over twelve thousand years ago. It is believed that he originally arrived in America by way of the Bering Straits, possibly fifteen to twenty-five thousand years ago, and that migrations continued until fairly recent times. The main path was probably down through central Canada to the Great Plains, spreading thence east and west, and south into Central and South America. Eminent archaeologists are attempting to trace the migrations: bits of evidence are turning up in ancient campsites, road excavations, through professional and amateur discoveries. Some day this story may be complete; today it is but a theory supported by some concrete data.

The earliest dated trace of man on the Columbia was uncovered by Dr. L. S. Cressman on the Oregon side of the river at the head of the Long Narrows near The Dalles. Dr. Cressman's crew sank their excavations through thirty feet of midden, which is what the trained digger calls what is known to the amateur as "camp dirt," and is the refuse left behind by the prehistoric occupants. The upper horizons contained trade goods marking the coming of the white man, the oldest produced bones of extinct animal life, crude implements, and ancient fire pits, dated by the "carbon 14" method at 9,785 years ago, plus or minus 200 years. There is much of this type of evidence that is disappearing beneath the waters. Already dams like Bonneville, The Dalles, McNary, Rock Island, Chief Joseph, and Grand Coulee have buried long stretches of the Columbia, and soon the John Day, Priest Rapids, Wanapum, and Rocky Reach will complete the flooding of the original channel.

For variety and abundance of Indian artifacts no area in the United States exceeds the Columbia River. Every bar and island is a storehouse, and few are the places one can walk along her shores without seeing traces of the past.

The reason for this concentration of populations along the river, and the consequent enrichment of the area with artifacts, was the great abundance of salmon for food. It is difficult for one who did not see them, to visualize the hordes of salmon that once migrated up the mighty river from early spring to late fall, to reproduce and later to die in the lakes and streams of the river's many sources. First came the Chinook, lord of fishes, followed by the bluebacks, silvers, steelhead, and last the fall run of Chinook and lesser species. By the millions they came, fighting their way up the turbulent Columbia for hundreds of miles. Paul Kane, the artist, wrote in 1847 about Kettle Falls, "The chief told me he had taken as many as 1700 salmon, averaging 30 pounds each, in one day. None of these salmon ever return to the sea but remain in the river and die by the thousands." They start upstream fat and oily, consuming themselves on the long journey; for they take no food after leaving the ocean, so that by the time they reach the upper river they are but shadows of their former selves, their poor noses all bent and their sides bruised from the rocks in the rapids. The natives therefore traveled downstream as far as they dared to obtain the choicer fish.

Sir George Simpson said in 1824 "the native population on the banks of the Columbia River is much greater than in any other part of North America that I have visited as from the upper Lake to the Coast . . . the shores are actually lined with Indian Lodges...at the Fishing Season."

Fish could be taken any place along the river, but the best places were the rapids and falls, for there the salmon would rest awhile in the eddies and could be taken easily with the scoop net, or they would leap the falls and be caught in traps. So thick did they concentrate in the pools below falling waters that merely by thrusting the spear into the deeps they could be taken. Umatilla Rapids, Priest Rapids, Rock Island Rapids, and Kettle Falls were all famous fishing places, as were the Long Narrows, near The Dalles, Oregon, and the Cascades, 40 miles downstream, and Celilo Falls, 15 miles above. Best of all was the Long Narrows, and it is here that more artifacts have been recovered than at any other place; it was also the great trade mart of the west. With the coming of the white man the Celilo Falls became the most famous of all places; for here the commercial fishermen improved fishing by blasting out channels and erecting cableways so the best pools could be easily reached. But in early days it was never as productive as the Long Narrows.

In that long meandering reach of the river, between the Cascades and the mouth of the Snake, most of the archoeological sites lie on the north side. There are two reasons for this, one is that the north side, being more exposed to the sun, eroded much faster, and there are more passes through the cliffs and more places convenient for camping . On the south side for long distances the cliffs rise vertically from the waters edge. The other reason is that the tribes came mostly from the north and northeast, and as they were constantly at war with the Snake Indians to the south; there was no reason to cross the river and expose themselves to attack. There were, however, several large and important sites on the south side, notably at the Deschutes River, The Dalles, and the John Day River.

Archaeological sites along the river are far too numerous to tabulate here; there are hundreds of them, and only the most prominent can be mentioned. Some of the largest have been eroded away within the past hundred years, great numbers must have disappeared over the centuries. And some, close to the river, have been covered by the silts of floods, and the wanderings of the river have left them far from its banks; these will some day be uncovered. Mr. N. G. Seaman says that some places the river is a mile from where it was when first surveyed in the mid-1800's. While hunting on the lower river, one can trip over the top strands of fences all but covered by flood silt. Each year the Columbia rises in flood ten to twenty feet, subsequent erosion of the banks uncovers the old camp grounds and exposes the relics, which will be washed away and lost forever in the next high water.

Fig. 1

ANCIENT VILLAGE SITE ON THE COLUMBIA RIVER
The depressions in the foreground are house pits.

An Indian village site can be easily identified, especially if the river is cutting away the edges. The soil will be deep black and full of pieces of broken rock that appear to be burned, cooking rocks that shattered when heated and dropped into baskets of water used for boiling food. There will be bits of bone, ashes, charcoal, and flint chips. And if you are lucky, maybe an arrowhead or two, or a stone pestle.

Most village sites are in the shape of small mounds,

centuries of occupancy accumulated enough refuse to elevate the area. Fortunately for archaeologists and relic hunters, the natives were indescribably filthy. Refuse was simply cast on the floor or out the door; sanitation was completely unknown. The odor from it all enveloped the village like a solid atmosphere. It has been said the smell of the distant Clatsop Indian town reaching Astoria on the wings of the warm southwest spring breeze, was the origin of the expression "Chinook wind." Native houses were crowded and dark, and many artifacts were dropped and became covered with refuse. Some artifacts were obviously buried. Perforated sinkers have been found in caches of half a dozen, to thirty or forty. Perhaps a native hid his treasures before leaving on a hunting trip which became a prehistoric tragedy, and he never returned to reclaim them. Or a sudden flood might cover a village with silt. Over the centuries a village site would become saturated with artifacts.

ASTORIA TO SAUVIES ISLAND

From Astoria, Oregon to Washougal, Washington, the Columbia flows majestically through a wide rich valley. Annual floods prevented the dense fir forest from encroaching on the low level plains; dikes now prevent the floods from covering the plains turned into prosperous dairy and truck farms. The river varies from one to four miles in width; the tide affects the flow as far upstream as Bonneville Dam. The broad valley supported a forest of oak, ash, and other hardwoods and an astonishing variety of small plants which in turn sustained and nourished a multitude of animal life. "Slept but very little last night for the noise kept up during the whole of the night by Swans, Geese, White and Grey Brant Ducks etc.—they are emensly noumerous and their noise horid," complained Lt. Clark of their camp opposite the outlet of the Willamette River. It was a paradise for the Indians, this lower river valley, for the climate was mild and food was plentiful.

About the mouth of the Columbia were several Indian villages, now mostly washed away. On the Washington side near Point Ellice was the main village of the Chinooks, called Quatsa'mts, from which in 1800, the one-eyed potentate Concomly ruled all the surrounding country. The first white people to see this town were from the *Columbia Rediviva*, Capt. Robert Gray commanding, discoverer of the Columbia River in 1792. John Boit recorded in his log: "May 12, N. Latt. 46° 7' W. Long. 122° 47'. This day saw an appearance of a spacious harbour abrest the Ship, haul'd our wind for itt, observ'd two sand bars making off, with a passage between them to a fine river. Out pinnace and sent her in ahead and followed with the Ship under short sail, carried in from ½ to 7 fm., and when over the bar 10 fm. Water quite fresh. The river extends to the NE as far as eye cou'd reach, and water fit to drink as far down as the bars, at the entrance. We directed our course up this noble river in search of a village. The beach was lin'd with natives, who ran along shore following the ship. Soon after, about 20 canoes came off, and brought a good lot of furs and salmon, which last they sold two for a board nail. The furs we likewise bought cheap, for copper and cloth. They appeared to view the ship with the greatest astonishment and no doubt we was the first civilized people that they ever saw. At length we arriv'd opposite to a large village, situate on the north side of the river about 5 leagues from the entrance, came to in 10 fm. sand, about ¼ mile from the shore. The river at this place is about 4 miles over. We purchas'd 4 Otter skins for a sheet of copper, Beaver skins, 2 spikes each, and other land furs, 1 spike each. May 18. Shifted the Ship's berth to her Old Station abrest the Village Chinoak, command'd by a chief name Polack. Vast many canoes full of Indians from different parts of the river were constantly alongside. Capt. Gray named this river Columbia's and the North entrance

tants, more than the present town of Ridgefield.

A small stream called Lake River, the outlet of Vancouver Lake, flows past this site, and on its banks were four other large villages and several small ones; in each of the large ones the outlines of the former houses can still be seen plainly. Three of the sites are yet untouched, although a great many relics have been picked up as the water washes them out of the banks. Lewis and Clark called the tribe Shoto, although it is likely that they misunderstood their informer, who probably tried to tell them that Soto lived there. Soto was the son of a Spaniard called by the natives Kanope, one of the survivors of a shipwreck spared by the Indians because of his knowledge of working iron, who married a native woman. What a story he could have written!

Fig. 3

CACHE OF PERFORATED SINKERS, SAUVIES ISLAND

About Lake River are numerous ponds and channels, all of which show signs of occupancy, and have produced many relics. On the western shore of Vancouver Lake is a site (CL 5) that is washing away and appears to be very old. Arrow points and stone pieces are quite crude. Crudeness is no evidence of age, but no bone is found in this site, and bone will last for centuries, in the damp, alkaline soil. The more modern sites are full of broken deer, elk, and other game bones. There are other villages with this "old" look on the lower river, and on Sauvies Island. In these the structure of the midden is different from those known to be quite modern.

SAUVIES ISLAND

Sauvies Island lies at the junction of the Willamette River with the Columbia. It is about 16 miles long and five wide at the center, with an area of nearly 40 square miles. It is low and flat and was once open woodlands in-

Fig. 4

WAPPATO

terspersed with small and large lakes. The soil is extremely rich, the island is now diked and covered with numerous and prosperous farms.

This wilderness setting offered a beautiful residential site for the Indians. While practical considerations alone determined the selection of a native village site—its prox-

imity to food and fuel, and to the river—the savage heart
must have been delighted by the picturesque beauty of
Sauvies Island. Groves of imposing oaks shaded the wide
meadows, ornamented with wild roses and buttercups,
fragrant cottonwoods lined the banks of the quiet waters.
The rivers and lakes teemed with fish and waterfowl, but
is was wappato, or Indian potato, that made the natives
on the island wealthy; for not only did the wappato pro-
vide an ample supply of food for the residents—it also
could be traded up and down the river. For it grew in
abundance only in the area near the Willamette River,
and all Indian tribes were very fond of it.

Because food was close at hand, food that was abundant
except in the very early spring, the natives of Sauvies
Island and the lower river could and did live in large
permanent villages. These were always built on the edge
of a river or lake. The Indians had little fear of attack
by enemies, and did not need to conceal their towns. The
houses were large and comparatively well built, each containing several families, and arranged along the bank in
rows, with many canoes pulled up on the shore in front.
Throughout every village swarmed innumerable children and dogs. The women were always busy, making
mats or preparing wappato or salmon. Like women
throughout the ages, their work was never done. Except
when engaged in hunting, fishing, or making a canoe, the
men lolled about enjoying the sunshine or engaged in
gambling or conversation. Slaves did all the menial work,
if the head of the house was wealthy enough to own one
or two. Warfare was very infrequent, generally conducted
only to acquire a fresh supply of slaves.

Alexander Ross, with the Astor expedition in 1811,
gives an interesting description of an Indian village: "On
a fine day it is amusing to see a whole camp or village,
both men and women, here and there in numerous little
bands, gambling, jeering and laughing at one another,
while groups of children keep in constant motion, either
in the water or practicing with bow and arrow, and even

the aged take a lively interest in what is passing, and there appears a degree of happiness among them, which civilized men, wearied with care and anxious pursuits, perhaps seldom enjoy."

No one knows how long Sauvies Island was occupied. Certainly not for thousands of years like—for instance—the Long Narrows for the island, geologically speaking, is very young. It was formed by the Columbia and Willamette Rivers meeting against a ledge of rock, part of which can be seen at the lower end and is known as Warrior Rock, causing the waters to decrease in velocity and lose part of their load of silt. It is in a constant state of change, washing away in one place and building up in another, now retarded by jettys and dredging.

At the same time, it is known that it was occupied for many hundreds of years. In some places the mounds of accumulated refuse are ten or more feet. Fireplaces are frequently seen on the banks covered with a deep layer of silt over which a rich soil has been built up by decaying vegetation and in which stand groves of large oak trees. There are signs of old sloughs and channels that have silted in, and been dry for ages. At all of these places camp rock can be found.

There are at least fifteen large village sites on the island. The most famous was the Multnomah village (MU 2) on the northwest shoulder, now covered with dredged sand and known as Reeder's beach. Lewis and Clark passed this town on March 30, 1806, on their return trip. Capt. Lewis says in his journal: "We passed several fishing camps on Wappatoe (Sauvies) Island, and at the distance of 5 miles above quathlahpootle (Batchelor's) island on the N.E. side we halted for breakfast near the place we had encamped on the evening of the 4th of November last; here we were visited by several canoes which came from two towns situated a little distance above us on Wappatoe Island. The first of these tribes about 2 miles above call themselves Clan-nah-quah, the other about a mile above call themselves Mult-no-mah. From these visitors we purchased a sturgeon and some wappatoe and pashequa for which we gave some small fishing hooks. These like the natives from below are great higglers in dealing."

In their "Estimate of the Western Indians", Lewis and Clark observed: "Mult-no-mah Tribe reside on Wap-pa-tow Island in the mouth of the Multnomah, the remains of a large nation, 6 houses, probable number of souls, 800. Clan-nah-quah's tribe of Multnomah's on Wappato Island below the Multnomars, 4 houses, probable number of souls, 130." The Clan-nah-quah site (MU 1) is now nearly all washed away, only a bank of broken camp rock on the river shore marks the place.

The Multnomah village site has probably yielded more artifacts than all the other sites on the island, for it was very large and a great deal of it has washed away, leaving the relics exposed on the shore. When the white man first came to the island all the natives had died in the

Fig. 5

(McLure collection, photo by Howard Galbraith)
CARVED STONE, SAUVIES ISLAND

pestilence of 1830-35, and grass and brush had overgrown the area. In clearing the land, all the utensils that the Indians had used were lying on or near the top of the ground. The midden is several feet deep and rich in artifacts all the way down. The stone work is the very finest, and many beautiful long colored arrow points have been found, as well as carved bone pieces. Banded and perforated sinkers could be picked up by the hundreds. Mr.

Reeder has a large collection that came from his front yard. The Multnomah village was the locale of the novel *"Bridge of the Gods"* by Frederic H. Balch.

Another f a m o u s village was Cath-lah-min-na-min (CO 9) on the Willamette Channel side of the island, at the Multnomah-Columbia county line. Most of this site is now covered by the dike, but a considerable part of it is still exposed, although covered by a farmstead. Many of the Indian village sites have a farm house and barn built in the center of them. This is natural, for when the island was first settled the old camp sites would be relatively clear, requiring little preparation for building. And they were generally located in the most convenient places. Lewis and Clark say that Cath-lah-min-na-min had 12 houses and 280 inhabitants, it must have been a great deal larger than this before the smallpox epidemic about 1780, for the site covers several acres.

Gabriel Franchére, one of the original Astor party, gave a vivid description of this town. Three of the Canadian engagees of the Astor party, growing tired of a diet of nothing but dried fish, stole a canoe and attempted to return to Canada. Franchére with a party started in pursuit, going as far as the Cascades without sighting them. On their return trip they heard that the escapees were being held as slaves at the Cath-lah-min-na-min village and returned there to pick them up. Franchére continues:

"In the evening we arrived near the village where our deserters were, and saw one of them on the skirts of it. We proceeded to the hut of the chief, where we saw all three, more inclined to follow us than to remain as slaves among these barbarians. We passed the night in the chief's lodge, not without some fear and some precaution; this chief having the reputation of being a wicked man, and capable of violating the rights of parties. He was a man of high stature and good mien, and proud in proportion, as we discovered by the chilling and haughty manner in which he received us. Farnham and I agreed to keep watch alternately but this arrangement was superfluous, as neither of us could sleep a wink for the infernal thumping and singing made by the medicine men all night long, by a dying native. I had an opportunity of seeing the sick man make his last will and testament; having caused to be brought to him whatever he had that was most precious, his bracelets of copper, his bead necklace, his bow and arrows and quiver, his nets, his lines, his spear, his pipe, etc., he distributed the whole to his most intimate friends, with a promise on their part, to restore them if he recovered.

"On the 22nd, after a great deal of talk, and infinite quibbling on the part of the chief, we agreed with him for the ransom of our men. I had visited every lodge in the village and found but few of the young men, the greater part having gone on a fishing excursion; knowing, therefore, that the chief could not be supported by his warriors, I was resolved not to be imposed upon, and as I knew where the firearms of the fugitives had been deposited, I would have them at all hazards; but we were obliged to give him all our blankets, amounting to eight, a brass kettle, a hatchet, a small pistol, much out of order, a powder-horn, and some rounds of ammunition; with these articles placed before him in a pile, we demanded the men's clothing, the three fowling-pieces, and their canoe, which he had caused to be hidden in the woods. Nothing but our firmness compelled him to accept the articles offered in exchange; but at last, with great reluctance, he closed the bargain, and suffered us to depart with the prisoners and property."

While returning to Astoria the party encountered a violent storm, from which they were so glad to escape with their lives that the three prisoners went unpunished, thus closing the story with a happy ending.

A remarkable feature of this village was a large stone image erected in it. Sir George Simpson says "The Island contains, in its interior, a block of black basalt, rudely chiseled by the Indians of ancient days into a column of four or five feet in height and three in diameter." The natives believed, as did the early settlers, that to touch the stone would bring rain. Sir Simpson tells how one of his men once tried to move the stone, and that evening a violent storm descended on the area, thus vindicating the legend. The stone was still standing in 1880 when a reporter for the Portland *Oregonian* described it. Mr. Seaman says that the original settler on the site, growing tired of plowing around the image, rolled it onto a stone boat and dumped it into the Willamette Channel, where it still lies.

Fig. 6

AMATEURS DIGGING IN THE CATHALHMINNAMIN SITE, SAUVIES ISLAND

Members of the Oregon Archaeological Society were permitted to excavate on this site for two week-ends by the owner, Mr. Fred Cholick, in an area being prepared for a lawn. A number of arrow points and bone tools were found, and a fragment of a "slave killer." One excavator went down seven feet in the midden with no indication of approaching bottom. Oddly enough, not a single fishing implement was uncovered, while in a site one mile downstream (CO 7) these were found in profusion. This is characteristic of several sites along the river, it is probable that villages were occupied by the same tribes at different times of the year, as the artifacts found are those applicable to the season. Lewis and Clark and others state that it was necessary to change villages because of the enormous number of fleas that accumulated during a few months occupancy of a village.

A unique site (MU 11) near the Sauvies Island bridge, due to some geological phenomena is under water except at low tide and very low stages of the river. This is one of the few places along the river where perishable articles like baskets, rope, and wood implements may be found, as they are preserved by constant immersion in water. Along the bank are still visible storage pits lined with hemlock boughs, some of them containing acorns. Several woven and twined baskets have been found there, one was still full of acorns. Other artifacts occasionally picked up are bows, arrows, cedar bark rope, wood wedges, and fragments of canoe paddles, wooden bowls and spoons, and matting. Howard Galbraith found a complete cedar bark skirt there. Upon exposure to the air it disintegrated. The site is prehistoric, as no trade goods have ever been found there.

On the lower end of the road on the Columbia River side of the island is a site commonly called Henreici's but known to the Indians as Namuit (CO 5); it has washed completely away, but large collections were made from it during the early part of the century as the river was cutting into it. The camp rock, consisting of broken cooking and work stones, lies several inches deep on the shore, and banks of it extend for a quarter of a mile. By combing these rocks arrow points are sometimes found, badly scarred by the rolling rocks. This was once a very large village and must have been quite old, for traces of fire are found eight or more feet deep beneath the silt. Lewis and Clark show this town on their map but do not mention it.

There is an interesting and well authenticated story about one of the collections made on Sauvies Island. One of the early settlers built his home on the deserted site of one of the larger villages. In clearing the land numerous artifacts were found, and the wash from passing steamboats and the yearly flood eroded more from the banks.

This man picked up and saved the best of them and eventually accumulated a large collection of exceptionally fine stone and bone carvings and chipped pieces. Growing old and not wanting his collection to become dispersed, and as there was then no local museum to donate it to, he buried it in one of his fields. There it yet lies, the best single private collection of Indian work in the west. Some day it may again erode from the bank.

Fig. 7

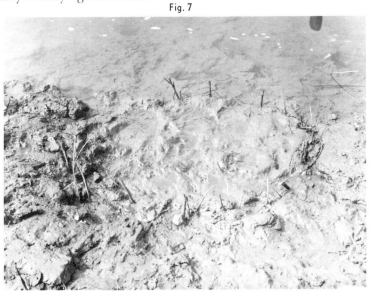

STORAGE BASKET IN SITU, DROWNED VILLAGE ON SAUVIES ISLAND

While the permanent village sites offer the best hunting grounds for relics, the entire island is rich because the natives for centuries traveled from considerable distances to harvest the wappato on its lakes. Traces of temporary camps can be found all along the lake shores, and in places where ponds and lakes have filled and disappeared. Many arrows were lost while hunting, especially in the old lake beds, some of which have been diked and drained. Any rocks found on the island, except along the "backbone" of the original rock ledge on which the island was built, are Indian rocks, carried in for camp and cooking stones.

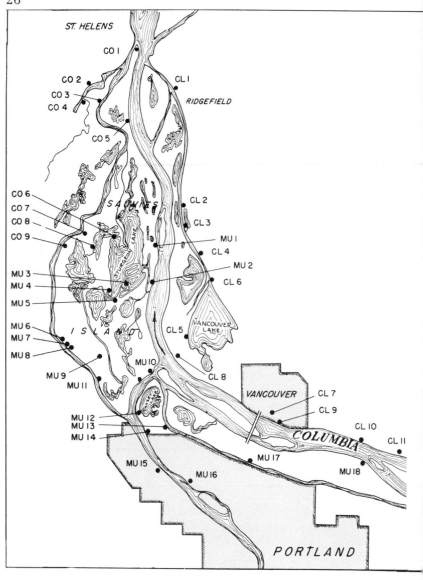

ST. HELENS

CO 1

CO 2

CO 3
CO 4

CL 1

RIDGEFIELD

CO 5

CO 6
CO 7
CO 8
CO 9

SAUVIES

CL 2

CL 3

MU 1
CL 4

STURGEON LAKE

MU 3
MU 4

MU 5

MU 2

CL 6

MU 6
MU 7

MU 8

ISLAND

CL 5

VANCOUVER
LAKE

MU 9

MU 11

MU 10

MU 12
MU 13

MU 14

CL 8

VANCOUVER

CL 7

CL 9

CL 10

COLUMBIA

CL 11

MU 17

MU 15

MU 16

MU 18

PORTLAND

STONE AGE CAMP SITES

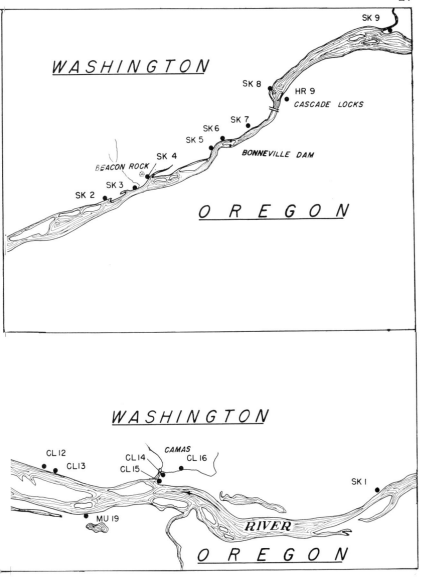

ALONG THE COLUMBIA RIVER

The wappato is the plant known as the "arrowhead," and is found in many parts of the United States. It is sometimes cultivated, especially by the Chinese, for food. The botanical name is *Sagittaria latifolia*, the name "wappato" is Indian. The edible part is a tuber about the size of a pigeon's egg, growing in the soft mud of lake and river shores. It cannot be pulled up because the root stalk is easily broken. The natives harvested it by wading into the water and loosening the bulbs with their toes, throwing them into a small canoe made for the purpose. On the shores they were dug with a pointed stick. What a hard way to make a living! But it was the chief food of thousands of Indians.

The wappato is no longer plentiful, but there are several places where it can still be found in quantity, and some people dig the tubers and eat them. There is, at this writing, a large patch on the east side of Highway 99 near the Kalama River, and wappato can frequently be seen in the lowlands on the Oregon side, around and below St. Helens. On Sauvies Island the great fields are gone , on some of the isolated ponds a few plants may occasionally be found. The tuber tastes something like a potato, plus a slightly nutty flavor.

INDIAN VILLAGE SITES
ON THE LOWER COLUMBIA

Some of the ancient sites shown on this map have disappeared under the advance of civilization. Some have been entirely eroded away, floods and the wash from passing ships takes yearly toll of others. A few, a very few, are intact, undisturbed since desertion by their stone age inhabitants—some during the great pestilence of the 1830's, and some centuries before from some unrecorded tragedy, a fire, perhaps, or destruction by an enemy, or failure of the salmon. None of the village ruins has ever been scientifically investigated to unlock the secrets they contain; a few more years and they must be all gone. On Sauvies Island, during the past thirty years, practically all of the numerous, large, rich sites, occupied for centuries, mounded up with the accumulations of refuse from generations of inhabitants, have vanished, most of them beneath the dike that encircles a large portion of the island. White residents, generally, are unconcerned and unknowing, not recognizing these landmarks in their midst. Not until they are all gone will it be realized that at least one should have been preserved intact as a historical monument, a cultural heritage and a tourist attraction.

The village names and population data listed here are from Lewis and Clark's Journals, unless otherwise noted. They made the only maps, from actual observation, showing Indian villages on the Columbia. Some they saw and visited, the locations and names of others were obtained from information and sketches drawn by the Indians, using a coal on deer skin or just a finger tracing in the sand. Their maps are remarkably accurate, considering the difficulty of the language barrier.

All the sites on this map are known to local amateur archaeologists. I have hunted over all of them except those that have disappeared. The locations of these were shown to me by "relic hunters" who knew them in the old days. The Lewis and Clark villages have been identified by their location on their maps, and bits of information from other early journals such as Alexander Henry and Franchére, and the work of the contemporary Portland historian, J. Neilson Barry, and others. There are no historical data on villages not named, most of them were deserted before the white invasion. Some are covered in more detail in the text.

CO 1. Warrior Rock, a canoe burial site and the rock ledge against which Sauvies Island was formed.

CO. 2. Clackstar, largest village on the lower Columbia. 28 houses and 1200 inhabitants. This seems to have been the home village of the famous Chief Keasno. It is now a cultivated field. No excavation has ever been done here, but many artifacts have been recovered from the plowed fields.

CO 3. Cath-lah-cum-up, six houses, 450 inhabitants. An old, deep site, now covered with a farmstead. On this site, where the edge is washed away, are found "slave killers" and other fine carvings, and many arrow points.

CO 4. An old village, prehistoric, at the outlet of Scappoose Creek.

CO 5. Namuit (Sir George Simpson). Lewis and Clark show two houses here, but do not mention the name of the town. Originally a very large village, it is now completely washed away. Banks of camp rock extend for a quarter of a mile along the river bank. Large collections were made from it as it was eroding away about the turn of the century. The coming of paddlewheel steamboats started the erosion of some of these towns, because of the large wave they threw up.

CO 6. A prehistoric site on the edge of Sturgeon Lake.

CO 7. "Pump House Site," two houses. Although trade articles were found here, and it must be historic, no early journals mention this town. It may have been part of CO 9, a short distance upstream. This place was partially excavated by members of the Oregon Archaeological Society, and reported in *Screenings*, Vol. 4 No. 3.

CO 8. This was once a large, prehistoric site, now entirely ruined by the dike. Early searchers report that this was one of the largest and richest sites on the island. It was called the "Bull Neck."

CO 9. Cath-lah-min-na-min, 12 houses, 280 inhabitants, now covered by the dike and a farmstead. This site covers several acres. It was here that Franchére rescued the voyagers being held as slaves.

MU 1. Clan-nah-quah, 4 houses, 130 inhabitants. Now all washed away and difficult to locate.

MU 2. Multnomah, 6 houses, 800 inhabitants, originally much larger. The most important site on the island, although most of it has washed away. This was the locale of the novel *"Bridge of the Gods."* It is now covered by a farmstead; it is supposed to be the main village of the Multnomah branch of the Chinooks, partially decimated by the smallpox epidemic about 1780, and completely decimated by the great pestilence.

MU 3. Prehistoric site on Sturgeon Lake, now all washed away. Favorite relic hunting area 40 or 50 years ago.

MU 4. A small, prehistoric site.

MU 5. A small site, probably used temporarily by the Tualatin Indians and others who came here to dig the wappato.

MU 6. Cath-la-nah-qui-ah, six houses and 400 inhabitants. Nathaniel Wyeth built Fort William near this town, but the residents had all died in the pestilence by then. Dr. McLaughlin had the houses burned. Excavations reveal everything covered with a film of cedar charcoal.

MU 7. The site of Wyeth's Fort William.

MU 8. One of the prehistoric sites that appears to be very old. There are no game or fish bones, and the midden has a different character from the more recent sites.

MU 9. Another "old" site, in 1958 being excavated by the Oregon Archaeological Society.

MU 10. A prehistoric site, now covered by a farm and no longer visible.

MU 11. The "drowned village." Preserved by constant immersion in water, wooden and fiber artifacts are found in this prehistoric village.

MU 12. A prehistoric site, no longer visible.

MU 13. The St. Johns site, a large village. Lewis and Clark show houses here, but do not name it.

MU 14. Ne-mel-quin-ner, four houses and 200 inhabitants. Before being covered by dredging and harbor improvements, this was called "the mouth of Gatton's Slough", a favorite haunt of early relic hunters.

MU 15. Covered by the plant of the Portland Gas and Coke Company.

MU 16. A small site no longer visible. The late Robert

H. Miller, an enthusiastic collector and student of Indian lore, said that the burial ground for this village was on the campus of the University of Portland.

MU 17. The Woodlawn site. Once a very large village, it was entirely carried away for fill material for a dike. This site was occupied after the white invasion, but not mentioned by any of the early writers.

MU 18. Ne-ei-cha-ke-oo, 24 mat lodges and one large wood house, a winter village of residents of the Cascades. Here Lt. Clark lit the port fire, and counted nearly 100 canoes. This site, now washed away, was near the Portland Airport.

MU 19. Ne-cha-co-kee, one house, 100 residents, the remains of a very large town decimated by the smallpox. An old chief here drew a map which was the basis for the Lewis and Clark map of the Willamette River and its branches.

CL 1. Quath-lah-pot-tle, 14 houses and 900 inhabitants, on the edge of Ridgefield, Washington. Nearly all early writers mention this town and say it extended for one quarter mile along the river bank. Lewis and Clark gave a medal to the principal chief. Remains of this town are still visible in a few places, but it is mostly all covered with flood silt.

CL 2. Village on Lake River, with a house pit 300 feet long.

CL 3. Village on Green Lake, now nearly all dug over by amateurs. Originally it contained four house pits.

CL 4. The largest site on Lake River, still intact, house pits visible.

CL 5. Another "old" site, nearly all washed away.

CL 6. Near the Felida moorage, on both sides of Lake River. House pits visible. (CL 2, 3, 4 and 6 were the "Shoto" villages.)

CL 7. Site of Fort Vancouver.

CL 8. The Wakanasi village, located by J. Neilson Barry but now lost. Mentioned only by Lt. Wilkes. Chief

Keasno moved to this village after losing nearly all of his slaves and relations in the great pestilence.

CL 9. Sketcu'txat (Spier and Sapir), now covered by the shipways and dock of the Vancouver Shipyard.

CL 10. Prehistoric site at the lower end of Image Road.

CL 11. Old site with pitted boulders.

CL 12. Fishers Landing, the "turtle bowl" is carved in the bedrock here.

CL 13. Ten Mile Tavern. Many carved boulders on the river bank.

CL 14. Prehistoric site partially covered by highway 830. One house pit excavated and reported in "Screenings", Vol. 4, No. 9.

CL 15. Several sites on both sides of Washougal River.

CL 16. Wagon Wheel Park site, eleven round house pits up to five feet deep. Reported on in "Screenings", Vol. 4, No. 10.

SK 1. Pictographs on the cliffs at Cape Horn.

SK 2. Marrs Landing, three very large house pits visible, several others covered by grading for a wharf. Carved boulder on the river bank.

SK 3. Wah-clel-lah. In 1806 there were 39 houses here. The site is now all washed away.

SK 4. Beacon Rock Moorage, part of a large site remaining.

SK 5. Garrison Eddy, large carved boulder and old village site.

SK 6. Clah-clel-lah, four houses. Present site of North Bonneville and Bonneville Dam.

SK 7. Vault site, and an old village, no signs now visible.

SK 8. Yeh-huh, 8 houses, now flooded by Bonneville Dam. The small island opposite SK 8 is Sullivan Island.

SK 9. Mouth of Wind River.

HR 9. Cathlackaty village (Henry). Still visible near the Columbia Hotel in Cascade Locks.

SAUVIES ISLAND TO THE DALLES

The Portland area had several large sites, now all gone except one. The largest was at the mouth Gatton's Slough (MU 14) below the St. Johns bridge, where many relics were picked up before the area was filled for industrial use. Other places are covered by the Portland Gas and Coke Co. plant and the Oregon Shipyards. The Vancouver Shipyard at Vancouver is built on a large village site that was called Sketcu'txat (CL 9).

The only one left in the vicinity of Portland is on the Columbia Slough near the St Johns Substation of the Bonneville Power Administration (MU 13). Some future archaeologist will have a frustrating time here, for this stone age site is being covered by the Portland Municipal dump. Another place on the Columbia Slough was one quarter mile east of Union Avenue (MU 17), it was entirely carried away for dike material. The late Robert H. Miller spent many days digging there and recovered a quantity of bone and stone artifacts. It was then known as the Woodlawn site and many boys now grown old, hunted arrow points there on a Sunday.

There was a village on the present site of the Portland Airport called Ne-er-cha-ke-oo (MU 18). Lieutenant Clark stopped there on his return from exploring the Willamette River. He wrote: "I landed at a large double house of the Ne-er-che-ki-oo tribe of the Shah-ha-la Nation, at this place we had seen 24 additional straw huts as we passed down last fall and whome as I have before mentioned, reside at the Great Rapids of the Columbia. On the bank at different places I observed small canoes which the women make use of to gather wappato and roots in the Slashes. Those canoes are from 10 to 14 feet long and from 18 to 23 inches wide in the widest part, tapering from the center to both ends and about 9 inches deep and so light that a woman may with one hand haul them with ease, and they are sufficient to carry a woman and some loading. I think 100 of these canoes were piled up and scattered in different directions about in the woods in the vicinity of this house, the pilot informed me that those canoes were the property of the inhabitants of the Grand Rapids who used them occasionally to gather roots. I entered one of the rooms of this house and offered several articles to the natives in exchange for wappato, they were sulky and positively refused to sell any. I had a small piece of port fire match in my pocket, off of which I cut a pece one inch in length & put it in the fire and took out my pocket compas and set myself down on a mat on one side of the fire, and a magnet which was in the top of my inkstand. the port fire cought and burned vehemently, which changed the colour of the fire; with the magnit I turned the needle of the compas about very briskly; which astonished and alarmed these natives and they laid several parsels of wappato at my feet, & begged of me to take out the bad fire; to this I consented; at this moment the match being exhausted was of course extinguished and I put up the magnet &c. this measure alarmed them so much that the womin and children took shelter in their beads and behind the men, all of this time a very old blind man was speaking with great vehemence, apparently imploring his god. I lit my pipe and gave them smoke, & gave the womin the full amount (value) of the roots which they had put at my feet". Port fire is a sort of fuse made of slow burning powder. This site was washed away, probably in a flood of 1810, as no other explorers mention it.

The town on the river near the western edge of Blue Lake below Troutdale was called Ne-cha-co-kee (MU 19), and consisted of one large house and the remains of several others. Lewis and Clark stopped there and "back of this house I observe the wreck of 5 houses remaining of a very large village, the houses of which had been built in the form of those we first saw at the long narrows of the E-lute Nation with whome those people are connected. I endeavored to obtain from those people of the situation of their nation, if scattered or what had become of the nativs who must have peopled this great town. an old man who appeared of some note among them and father to my guide brought forward a woman who was badly marked with the Small Pox and made signs that they all died with the disorder that marked her face, and which she was verry near dieing with when a girl. from the age of this woman this Destructive disorder I judge must have been about 28 or 30 years past, and about the time the Clatsops inform us that this disorder raged in their towns and distroyed their nation. Those people speak a different language from those below tho' in their habits and manners &c. they differ but little from the Quathlahpohtles. their women ware the truss as those do of all nations residing from the Quathlahpohtle to the entrance of Lewis's (Snake) river and on the Columbia above for some distance. those people have some words the same with those below but the air of their language is entirely different, their men are stouter and much better made, and their womin ware larger & longer robes than those do below; those are most commonly made of Deer skins dressed with the hair on them. they pay great attention to their aged. severall men and women whom I observed in this village had arived at a great age, and appeared to be helthy tho' blind. I provailed on an old man to draw me a sketch of the Multnomar River and give me the names of the nations resideing on it which he readily done, and gave me the names of 4 nations who reside on this river two of them very noumerous". When the dike was built through this site in 1940 heaps of crumbling bones were uncovered, probably the victims of the smallpox epidemic and the great pestilence.

On the Washington side of the Columbia there is one of the "old" sites (CL 10) at the foot of Image Road shortly above Vancouver. At Fishers Landing (CL 12) and one mile above, behind the Ten Mile Tavern (CL 13) are contemporary sites, now nearly washed away. At the Fisher site is the famous "turtle bowl", an effigy mortar carved in solid bedrock. Here too, is a large boulder covered with conical pits one to four inches in diameter. These pitted boulders are quite common on the lower river, nearly every place where there was a village near large rocks there are pits. No one has ever determined their purpose, although there are many theories, most of them as absurd as the popular notion that arrow points were made by dropping water on the heated stone. At the Ten Mile Tavern site are a number of boulders covered with random carvings and deep pits. This is the

Fig. 8

CARVED BOULDER, TEN MILE TAVERN SITE

only place where the deeply incised random lines appear. At the Image site, arrow points are practically non-existent, but fishing rocks are plentiful. At the Fishers and Ten Mile Tavern locations, all types of artifacts are found. At the latter site a beautifully carved steatite effigy was dug out of a flower garden. It had the shape of a bird with the face of a man, and showed definite Northwest influence. These places are so old that all bone has disappeared.

At the mouth of the Washougal River, in Camas, Washington, there were once many signs of Indian villages, but most have disappeared under the advance of civilization. In Wagon Wheel Park there is a practically undisturbed site (CL 16), containing eleven house pits up to four feet deep and 40 in diameter. The pits are round, indicating the semi-subterranean type house instead of the usual rectangular plank house. In this place, too, all bone has disappeared. Another site along Lackamas Creek on the edge of Camas has been dug over, and both sides of this creek show occupancy for a mile from its mouth. Fire pits are showing in the banks several feet beneath the surface.

Between Washougal and Skamania there is not much evidence of habitation for between is the famous Columbia River gorge where the river has plowed a furrow through the Cascade Mountains, whose great scenic beauty interested the natives not at all, for in the gorge there was neither game nor roots. At Skamania starts the heavily populated Cascades area, site of several villages and a good bit of rugged Oregon history. The Cascades was formed 700 years ago by an enormous slide from the mountains to the north, causing the river to alter its course, backing up its water nearly to the Long Narrows. The raised waters drowned out forests along its course, the stumps of which reached to the waters' surface and caused considerable trouble to navigation and much comment by early travelers. From two of these stumps, at different places in the river, Prof. D. B. Lawrence, of the University of Minnesota, sent samples to the University of Michigan, where the date, 700 years ago, was established by the "carbon 14" method. Frank Wilke of Bingen says that in times of extremely low water, which might occur every few years, ancient village sites would be exposed near Bingen, villages drowned out by the pool behind the slide. The artifacts found in them were similar to those found on the modern sites. Of course, all is now under many feet of water in the lake behind Bonneville Dam. Traces of the old river bed were found during geological explorations for Bonneville Dam, north of the present channel. The slide forced the river over against the cliffs on the south, causing it to tumble over the rocks, thus forming the Cascades.

The Reverend Gustavus Hines, while camped at the Cascades in 1843, described them: "Occasionally, however, we ventured out to the shore of the Columbia, contemplating her majesty, as she pours her exhaustless flood down the ledge of rocks which forms the beautiful cascades. The river here falls in continued rapids for three miles, not less than fifty feet. That portion of the rapids properly called the cascades, presents an appearance of grandeur and sublimity not inferior to that of the rapids of the Niagara river, above the great cataract. At this place the Columbia rushes through the cascade range of mountains, and the channel through which it pours its mighty torrent, appears not more than thirty rods wide, while each shore presents indubitable evidence that, by a vast accumulation of water above, these mountain barriers were torn asunder, and thus this mighty river found its way to the Pacific ocean. The Indians here have a tradition that, a long time ago, the mountain was joined together over the river, and that the river performed a subterraneous passage for some distance, with a slow current, and that their people used to pass up and down with their canoes without difficulty; but all at once the foundations of this mighty arch crumbled beneath their ponderous weight, and the whole mass came tumbling into the river, filling up the channel and quite damming up the stream, and thus were formed the beautiful cascades. The probability is that this tradition is true only in part. Doubtless the time was when there were no cascades here, and they were probably formed by the mountain's sliding into the river in tremendous avalanches, and thus filling the channel. The land on each side of the river at this place is rough and sterile, and the scenery wild beyond description. The cascades are fifty miles above Vancouver, and

Fig. 9

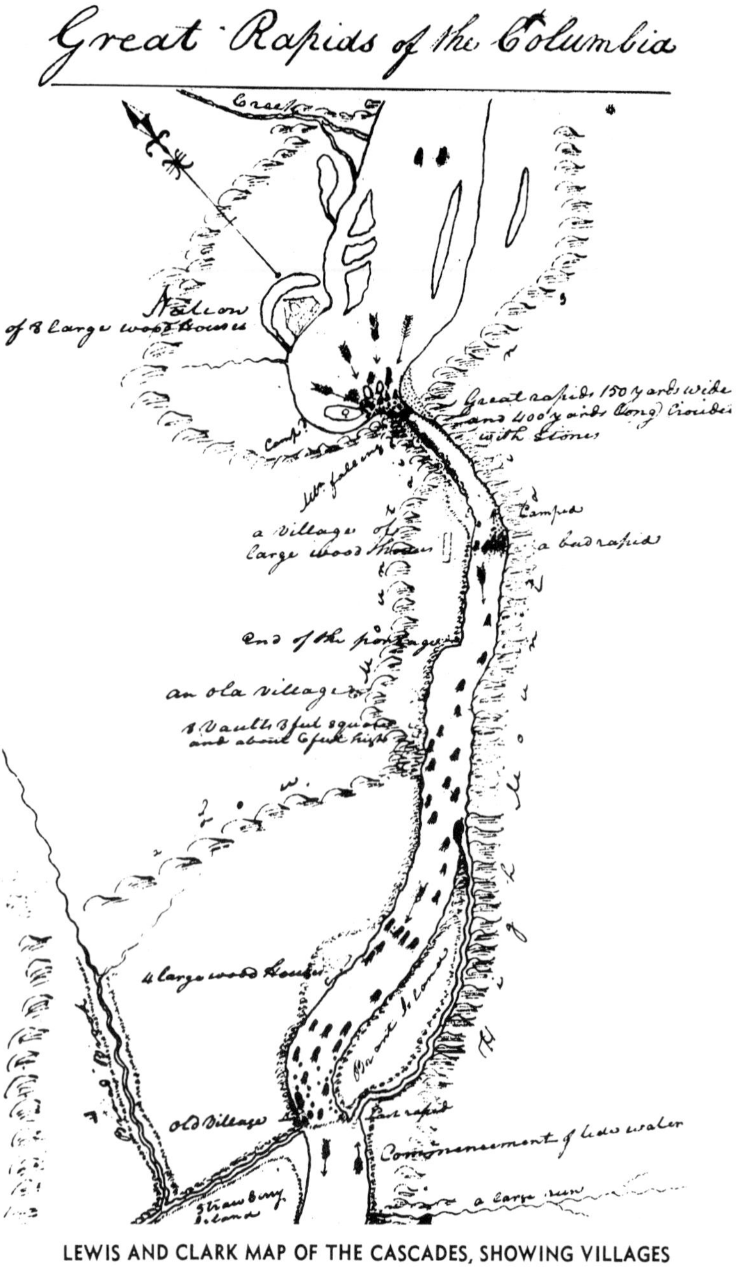

Great Rapids of the Columbia

LEWIS AND CLARK MAP OF THE CASCADES, SHOWING VILLAGES

one hundred and forty-five from the mouth of the Columbia."

The "mighty arch" was the mythical Bridge of the Gods which fell when Wy-east and Klickitat fought over the lovely Loo-it; geology proves that such a bridge could not have existed. It is only a partial myth, however, as it is likely that it was possible to cross the slide before it was topped by the river, which would have taken but a few hours. Of course, no one did, because the monstrous slide, probably preceded by a violent earthquake, would have so frightened the natives that they would have fled in terror. Then too, it is unlikely that there were any residing in the vicinity, as without the Cascades to form a good fishing place there would be no reason to reside in this rugged, stormy area. The slide may have been disastrous in more ways than one, if it formed a rough, swift section of the river it would have prevented the salmon from ascending, and the natives above would have starved, and four years later there would have been practically no salmon, either. Just such a situation was created on the Fraser River from blasting out a railroad cut, almost completely stopping the enormous salmon runs in that stream. At that time it was not known that after the water reached a certain velocity the salmon would not ascend it, and the runs were not restored until years later when fishways were built.

There were villages both above and below the Cascades, only one of which (SK 2) is relatively undisturbed, on the homesite of Mr. Arch Sams of Skamania. There are three large house pits remaining, and others were leveled off for a steamboat wharf known as Marr's Landing. One mile above was the large Wah-clel-lah village (SK 3), in 1806 consisting of 23 houses and the remains of ten others. This is sometimes called the Big Nose site, and is now practically all washed away.

The Lewis and Clark party stopped there on April 9, 1806, and noted in their Journals: "This village appears to be the wintering station for two bands of the shah-ha-la Nation. One band has already moved to the falls of the Multnomah (Oregon City) which is the place they take their Salmon. the other band is now moveing a fiew miles above to the foot of the rapid on this river, at which place they take their salmon. 14 houses only appear occupied and the inhabitants of those moveing off hourly, they take with them in their canoes independent of all their household effects the bark of their houses, and boards. 9 houses has been latterly abandoned and 14 others is yet thinly inhabited at present, and the remains of 10 or 12 others are to be seen and appears to have been enhabited last fall. those people were not hospital and with some dificuelty we precured 5 dogs and a fiew Wappato of them."

At the foot of Beacon Rock was a village site (SK 4) now nearly all washed away. There are a few traces of it below the railroad fill and the moorage is built on part of the washed deposit. At Garrison Eddy, just below Bonneville Dam is another (SK 5) ; on the edge of it is a rock carved with circle and dot designs. This was the lower end of the town of Lower Cascades, no sign of which remains except some timbers of the jail. The old portage road can still be traced through the woods. The Indian village Clah-clel-lah (SK 6) was on the place where North Bonneville was later built, and Yeh-huh (SK 8) was just above the rapids near the present plywood mill. In Cascade Locks the midden of a village (HR 9) can be seen next to the Columbia Hotel.

The natives of the Cascades were very troublesome to the early travelers. A party in 1811, after making the portage, assembled to embark near the Yeh-huh village. The Indians had pilfered several articles, including a suit of clothes belonging to a Mr. McLennan. As soon as they left that worthy gentlemen sailed his hat into the midst, saying, "Gentlemen, there's my hat; you've got the rest; the suit is now complete". In 1814, two canoes loaded with merchandise under the command of Alexander Stuart and James Keith, of the North West Company, with 15 men, were dispatched from Astoria to forts east of the mountains. Arriving at the foot of the Cascades, they commenced the portage. The natives, meanwhile, assembled in large numbers. One of them seized a parcel, and one of several Indians armed with bows and arrows aimed at Stuart, who raised his gun with a warning but received an arrow in his shoulder. He drew the trigger but the gun misfired, the priming being wet, and while repriming was severely wounded with an arrow in his side, which would have been fatal if it had not been deflected by a stone pipe in his pocket. At the same moment, his gun fired and shot the Indian dead. The natives rushed, but were driven back with the loss of one, killed with his own war club after being wounded. Soon several canoes of reinforcements came up, and Stuart and his party abandoned the cargo and escaped in one of their canoes. A large party returned from Astoria to retrieve the goods, but obtained only a small quantity, meanwhile paying dearly for subsistence from the very natives who robbed them.

The Cascades was the locale of much early Oregon history, especially during the boom times of the gold rushes to Idaho and Eastern Oregon in the 1860s. Earlier, in 1856, there was the Cascades massacre, a tragic battle with comic opera overtones, between white settlers and Indians.

Also on the north shore, about the mouth of Wind River, and near Bingen, are traces of native villages and there was a large town at the mouth of Klickitat River, with another two miles above. Opposite a small rock island in the river a few miles below The Dalles was a village of eight houses, all signs of which were destroyed by railroad construction, although a few artifacts are found on the banks after each spring flood.

THE LONG NARROWS

In all the world there is no place quite like the Long

Narrows of the Columbia. Also known as the Grand Dalles and Five Mile Rapids, this geological wonder was a barrier to navigation and a popular congregating place for the Indians of many tribes from up and down the river, and from the North and South as well. In this channel through the basalt the entire flow of the Columbia was compressed to a width of a couple of hundred feet. The violence of the current gouged out holes that are 175 feet below sea level, plucking out slabs of the jointed basalt with enough force to hurl them over the rim of the chasm. Swirling waters, using pebbles for tools, ground out vertical cylindrical holes one to twelve feet in diameter and many feet deep in the bedrock with the precision of the modern diamond drill. Each spring in flood stage the waters rose 45 or more feet, drowning out Celilo Falls 15 miles above and spilling over the rocky shores in a series of narrow channels. In flood stage it was a region of turbulence and violence that, once seen, could never be forgotten.

The early Hudson's Bay Company voyageurs called the place "Les Dalles", meaning the flag stones, a term referring to the wide expanses of washed bedrock. To them it was a region of great labor. All the freight had to be carried a distance of about one and a half miles over a rough, rocky trail, meanwhile protecting themselves and their baggage from the natives. Then the empty boats had to be towed up or let down through the channel with long cords, with a man or two in it to fend the boat away from the rocks. Mrs. Marcus Whitman, entering the country in 1836, described it thus: "This was done by attaching a strong rope of considerable length to the stern of the boat, two men only remaining in it to guide it and keep it clear of the rocks, while the remainder, and as many Indians as could be obtained, draw it along with the rope, walking on the edge of the rocks above the frightful precipice. At the Little Dalles, just above these, the current is exceedingly strong and rapid, and full of whirlpools. Not recollecting the place particularly, at the request of the bowsman I remained in the boat, being quite fatigued with my walk past the other Dalles. It is a terrific sight, and a frightful place to be in, to be drawn along in such a narrow channel, between such high, craggy, perpendicular bluffs, the men with the rope sometimes clambering upon their hands and knees upon the very edge, so high above us to appear small, like boys". The Long Narrows is five miles above the town of The Dalles, Oregon.

The boiling waters, and the numerous channels in the bedrock during flood season, made ideal places for taking the salmon, for they would swim close to the cliffs to escape the worst currents, and rest awhile in the backwaters and eddies where they could be easily netted. The number of salmon that formerly ascended the river is almost unbelievable. In one day in 1913, one of the Seufert Brothers fish wheels at the upper end of the Long Narrows dipped up 68,000 pounds of salmon, and this after the river had been fished commercially for decades with no thought of conservation. An Indian with his crude instruments could have taken about 100 fish a day, averaging 20 pounds each. Even as late as 1920 it was possible to catch nine blueback salmon, which are quite small and weigh only a few pounds each, with one dip of the net. Many tons of salmon were sold in later days by the Indian fishermen for one half to one cent a pound.

Astride the divide between the interior and coastal groups, and commanding the only water level pass between California and Canada, the Long Narrows became the great trade mart of the West, and the permanent residents were the middlemen in the traffic. The western Indians traded dried clams, dentalium shell, baskets, wappato, and wooden implements for furs, feathers, robes, dried fish, and slaves; all might be sold again further up or down the river.

More natives came to the Long Narrows to enjoy the festivities and the gambling than to fish, for the best fishing places were limited and individually owned, and fish could be caught at many other places on the river. Alexander Ross says: "The main camp of the Indians is situated at the head of the Narrows and may contain, during the salmon season, 3,000 souls, or more; but the constant inhabitants of the place do not exceed 100 persons, and are called Wyampams. The rest are all foreigners from different tribes throughout the country, who resort hither not for the purpose of catching salmon, but chiefly for gambling and speculation, not in fish, but in other articles."

But great quantities of salmon were taken and dried, pulverized, and stored in circular baskets two or three feet long and one in diameter, lined with dried salmon skins. Seven of these packs, which may have been of a standard size and value, were placed upright, with five more on top, then wrapped in mats; in this way the contents would keep for months. Lewis and Clark counted 107 of these stacks in the Long Narrows, containing 10,000 pounds of fish, and this was after everyone except the permanent residents had left. Another way to preserve the fish pemmican was to dig a hole in the ground, line it with straw and fish skins, pack it, and cover with earth. The dried fish was a favorite with the coast tribes, who could not preserve fish this way because of climatic conditions. The salmon, in preparing for drying, was split and the bones removed, then placed on racks in the sun and wind. It had to be continuously manipulated to expose the fresh interior as the outer layers dried. In the process it acquired a generous sprinkling of sand, for the winds in this area are violent. The sand caused the native's teeth to wear away rapidly. By middle age they were worn down to the gums, and in later life many of them suffered agonies of ulcerated teeth.

The large population and long occupancy made the Long Narrows the richest area, archaeologically, on the river, and perhaps in the whole United States. Every level place was used for a camp site, and in the loose sand many articles were lost. They could be screened out any place between Petroglyph Canyon and Big Eddy, although, of course, some places were much richer than others, where the favorite camping places and permanent villages were. According to the ethnologists Leslie Spier and Edward Sapir, there were nine village sites fronting the Long Narrows, three of them being on the Oregon side. Actually, the entire area was one big site, but there are five places which are of sufficient age and had enough use to accumulate large and deep middens. The villages of Spier and Sapir seem to be place names rather than towns. In 1805 the permanent village was known as Nix-luidix, and consisted of 21 large wood houses "in a Deep bend to the stard. side below which a ruggid black rock about 20 feet hiter they arc scattered permiscuisly on a elivated Situation near a mound of about 30 feet above the Common leavel, which mound has Some remains of houses and has every appearance of being artificial". This would place this important town, the Wishram of Washington Irving's *Astoria,* in the flat just above Wakemap mound, near the entrance of a small creek. Earl Marshall, who was there in 1903, said there was more indication of a village there than anywhere else; it was later completely destroyed by the construction of the railroad.

Fig. 10 shows the Long Narrows, taken in 1956 during construction of The Dalles dam (1). Big Eddy is at 2, the famous elk pictograph and a number of others are on the cliff north of the figure 2; some of them are above the level of the pool, and can still be seen from a boat. Grave Island is 3. Archaeological sites are 4, Maybe; 5, Congdon; 6, Indian Well; 7, Atlatl Valley; 13, Five Mile Locks; and 14, Big Eddy. Wakemap Mound shows plainly at 8, outlines of the trenches dug under the direction of Warren Caldwell may be observed across its top. The long flat at 9 was called Colowesh Bottom, after an Indian chief. It is the spill basin of a large waterfall that came over the cliff to the north in early geological times. There were many cremation pits and burial sites in this flat, and it was used extensively for habitations. Wishram

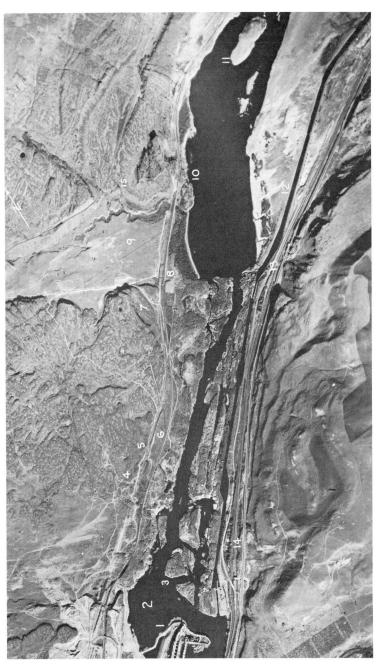

Fig. 10   AERIAL VIEW OF THE LONG NARROWS

legends say that here the different tribes met to contest in athletic games. It is now a lake. At 10 is Petroglyph Canyon, and 11 is Upper Memaloose Island. The Celilo Canal built in 1915 around the Long and Short Narrows and Celilo Falls is shown at 12. This picture was taken at low water stage, during flood the waters reach nearly to the base of Wakemap Mound and much of the channelled bedrock along the Narrows is covered. Not evident in this view are the high cliffs and rugged hills that surround the area.

In prehistoric times, long before the coming of the horse, one of the foot paths to the Long Narrows was down one of the rocky draws at No. 15 Fig. 10; the cliffs around Colowcah Bottom are a hundred feet or more high, and difficult to pass. The rocks on the bottom of this draw are worn smooth, on some that were used as steps the edges are rounded off by the thousands of bare and moccasined feet that passed that way. The curious can still see these marks of ancient man, by leaving highway 830 just after it passes over the small bridge over the ravine and following down the steep slope. On the cliffs beneath the bridge are several excellent pictographs.

One of the more interesting traces of the ancient village of Nixluidix and the migratory inhabitants of the Long Narrows was the children's slide, Fig. 11, which was on the western edge of the summer site of the town. On this sloping slab of basalt that had tumbled from the cliff above were worn two grooves over half an inch deep in the hard black rock, from many generations of happy Indian children sliding down its smooth surface. It shows that the stone age children were not too much different from those called civilized; they had their games and pleasures and sorrows just as modern children do. And what a perfect place to spend the summer! New acquaintances from distant lands to be made, warm pools in the washed bedrock in which to swim, miles of cliffs and canyons to explore and for playing hide and seek—and no school days looming ahead.

Another deep midden existed on the Oregon side at Five Mile Locks, directly opposite Wakemap Mound. Part of this, near the river, had a structure exactly like Wakemap, and was about 11 feet deep. Further back from the river Dr. Cressman's crew went down 30 feet through midden, uncovering the oldest dated site along the river. Still further back, at the base of the cliffs, was a large cremation and burial site superimposed on a camp ground, now directly under highway 30. This place had been dug over for years.

At the entrance of Celilo Canal was another site covering several acres, much disturbed by highway, canal, and railroad construction. Many relics were found there when the work was going on. The Congdon, Maybe, and Wakemap sites also had deep middens.

Wakemap Mound, Fig. 12, was 350 feet long and 270 feet wide, up to 20 feet deep, a heap of debris and refuse, the accumulation of centuries. Originally it was considerably larger, the railroad had cut through one side of it and a portage road took part of the other. Wakemap rhymes with wock-em-up and is a corruption of the Chinook word wuq'Emap which means ogress or old woman. Legend says that Wakemap was an ogress full of sharp stones who led amorous men to a painful death until Coyote with five long pestles succeeded in slaying her. Sharp flints and broken pestles were found by the hundreds in the mound.

In 1925 some scientific excavations of the mound were undertaken by the University of California and reported in "Archaeology of The Dalles-Deschutes Region," by Strong, Schenck, and Steward. For thirty years thereafter it remained untouched until construction work started on The Dalles dam, then "pot hunters" started digging, touching off the "Battle of Wakemap" between amateurs, bent on saving artifacts, and scientists, bent on saving information; fought with considerable vigor and scant honor until the tact and understanding of Dr. Douglas

Osborne, of the University of Washington, obtained a
truce and excavations were conducted in an orderly and

Fig. 11

THE CHILDREN'S SLIDE

scientific manner, to the benefit of both factions.

The first scientific excavations after those of the Uni-
persity of California in 1926 were started by Louis Caywood for the National Park Service in 1952, but consisted
of test pits only. In 1953 and 1954, Dr. Warren Caldwell
directed a crew that cut three trenches through the
mound, a meticulous endeavor that uncovered the stratification and artifact sequence from which he reconstructed the story of the mound and the cultural traits
of its inhabitants; one of the most important archaeological
investigations of the Columbia River area, and from
whose report the data on the mound included here is
taken. In 1955 and 1956, excavations were continued by
members of the Oregon Archaeological Society. All excavations were under the supervision of Dr. Douglas Osborne. Eventually about two-thirds of the mound was

Fig. 12

WAKEMAP MOUND
Over 2000 years accumulation of camp refuse.

sifted and thousands of artifacts recovered, the balance will be sacrificed to the wind swept waters of Lake Celilo behind The Dalles Dam, through which the top of the remainder of the mound protrudes.

Wakemap mound was one of the best stratified archaeological sites on the Columbia River. In layer on layer, the inhabitants left traces of their culture, a complete record dating back about 2000 years. With shovel and trowel, and in spite of the wind and dust, which, as anyone who dug there can attest, was enough to cause the stoutest heart to cringe, the story was unfolded. In the deepest Horizon, on the bedrock, the original inhabitants built their shelters of brush and matting, obtaining some protection from the severe winds by a rock outcropping; but why this particular location was chosen to the exclusion of better ones nearby will forever be a mystery. The inhabitants were few and lived by hunting and gathering; the important salmon industry was just starting. Bone was used for tools, knives were large and pentagonal, art was in its infancy. The river had not yet cut its deep channel, and the site was subject to flooding.

STRATIFICATION IN WAKEMAP MOUND

Gradually the camp debris accumulated, population increased, there seemed to be some climatic change. Flooding was less frequent, Horizon II commenced, fish were now taken in quantity by spearing and netting but hunting and seed gathering were still important. Sudden appearance of stone bowls and mauls showed outside influence, and the area was becoming an important trade center. The residents had enough leisure to pay some attention to personal adornment. The mound was assuming shape; it was now deep enough to construct semi-subterranean huts covered with earth, with consequent rapid increase in depth as the houses decayed, fell down, and were rebuilt. Cedar splints such as are used for holding fish open for drying appeared. Thus commenced the era in which the Long Narrows became an important fishing center.

In Horizon III the village had grown much larger and had assumed its role as the metropolis of the west. Its neighboring village on the opposite shore was also assuming an important postion, following Wakemap in its progress. Dip netting, by which the taking of fish became much more prolific, commenced, and hunting became of secondary importance. There was an increase in elaborate carved stone objects, the famous Columbia River art complex was now well established. There were many varieties of small, barbed and stemmed arrow points, and the knives became smaller, approaching the "mule ear" type. (Fig. 60.) Houses were definitely semi-subterranean, with superstructures supported by posts, the forerunner of the later plank house. It was a time of prosperity and expansion for Wakemap, a time of full development.

Horizon IV was a time of decay, a decrease in artifacts but an increase in variety, with a gradual exodus of the inhabitants. By 1800 the Mound was deserted, but the area was not. There was now the village of Nixluidix, although Wakemap was no more, the Long Narrows was still the most important trade mart of the west, the meeting place for tribes far and near, as it had been since Horizon II.

Members of the Oregon Archaeological Society and scientists from the University of Washington worked the mound for approximately four years, sifting at least 15,000 yards of midden and expending about 7000 man days of labor, to quote some very rough figures. Arrow points were found in quantities of from a dozen to 100 a day; 15 to 20 was about average. It took about 11 days of digging to get one good carved stone piece, and many were the complaints from those who got in their 11 days and some one else came along for the first time and got the carving. But they all look back now with fond memories, the dust and heat forgotten.

The Atlatl Valley site, Fig. 10, No. 7, so named because of the number of mysterious stone artifacts (Fig. 66), thought to be atlatl weights found there, was an area roughly circular and 150 feet in diameter at the base of a vertical cliff a few hunded yards west of Wakemap Mound. There were five large cremation pits there, dug over many years ago for the artifacts that they contained. These pits were used for some time before white contact and for a short time afterward; in one of them a few glass beads were found. Beneath the cremations was a layer of basalt slabs from the cliffs above, overlaying a stratum of water deposited silt two to five feet deep. It was between the rocks and in the silt beneath them that the artifacts were found.

The most plentiful artifacts, excluding arrow points, were chipped knives, about one in ten of these were made from petrified wood, the rest of various flints and semi-precious stones. Practically all were type NAa and NAb, Fig. 58, and of the finest workmanship. These knives, apparently, were made to be used unhafted, or wrapped with leather for a handle. The arrow points in general were quite large, mostly type SBa, one and a half to two and a half inches long, but examples of every type were found. The smaller ones were of the most exquisite workmanship and material, beautifully chipped, and with long tapering barbs. They sometimes occurred in caches of two or three to as many as 25. They had not been attached to arrows, but probably had been buried in a pouch, for when a cache was troweled out, although they might lay side by side, the points were not oriented in the same direction. About 1000 knives and four or five times as many arrow points were taken from this site.

Carved stone work and personal adornment were rare, two zoomorphic bowls were uncovered, and a few decorated mauls. Not over half a dozen stone beads and bangles were found. One of the atlatl weights was carved in the figure of an animal, and fragments of two similar ones were excavated. In one small area 19 large plain stone mortars were found, and a few other small ones were scattered throughout the site.

At least 150 so-called atlatl weights came from this place;they generally occurred in pairs. There were two types, the girdled stone and the perforated lead ore or galena weights. There might be two stone, one stone and one galena, or two galena weights together. The weight varied from one and a half ounces to ten, most averaged six or seven, and when found in pairs the weight of each might vary considerably, as there had been no attempt to secure a pair of near equal sizes. A great deal of labor had been expended in fashioning these stones. They were all of hard material selected for its beauty; spotted porphyry, quartizite, pipestone, and in colors black, red, green, white, purple, mottled and striped. All were beautifully formed and highly polished, some were decorated with incised lines.

There was not a single pipe found in the entire site, although there were a few fragments that may have come from the cremations. This is unusual in a Columbia River burial ground, for that is what this area was, and very old, as practically all skeletal material had disappeared. If there were any bone artifacts they had decayed away without a trace. Scattered throughout the site were a few bits of copper, nearly completely corroded away. One of these was tested and found to be pure copper with a trace of lead and silver, which indicates native and not smelted copper. Native copper is found in nuggets and flakes in Michigan and in some places in Canada and Alaska.

The Maybe site, Fig. 10, No. 4, was a low mound about 200 yards from the river on the Washington side near the lower end of the Long Narrows. It too was an ancient burial ground superimposed on a still more ancient camp site. Many amateurs believe that this camp was once close to the river and occupied before the Long Narrows was formed, when the river was a wide rapid over the bedrock through which eventually the narrow deep chasm of the Long Narrows was cut. The mound was covered with soil and grass beneath which were large blocks of basalt and smooth river boulders, and like Atlatl Valley just below and amongst the stones were the artifacts. The knives found were similar to those from Atlatl Valley, but there the similarity of artifacts ends. There were several pipes, all of the heavy tube type except two that were long elbow pipes made of a soft stone similar to that from which many of the eastern pipes are carved. There were none of the delicate steatite pipes commonly called the Columbia River tube and which came later. Many stone beads were found, all large. One variety was one and a half inches to two inches long and up to a half inch in diameter, tapering from the center towards each end. (Fig. 43.) Several square ones were found, up to four inches long and one-quarter inch in diameter. Bangles were made of steatite and pure graphite, practically all of the beads were made of green schist. Stone rings occurred in several different sizes, and nose ornaments (Fig. 63) were found in one small area. Two small zoomorphic carvings—one is shown in Fig. 40—were uncovered in the center of the mound, and on the edges were several of the large sculptured heads. Mauls, bowls, and pestles were rare; the most common artifacts were knives, beads, and arrow points. Several atlatl weights similar to those that came from Atlatl Valley were found, and in addition there were a few of the long tapering and perforated stone types, Fig. 66. There were, however, a number of rather crudely shaped stones, resembling the girdled atlatl weights, but not polished, being merely rounded pebbles, flat on the bottom and with a shallow, pecked groove. These may have been war club heads, but they had the general shape and size of the girdled weights.

At a depth of four feet in the center of the mound there was another layer that may have contained graves, but there was no sign whatever of skeletal material or artifacts, just patches of soil stained with red ochre a foot or so in diameter and five or six feet apart. Beneath these were signs of large camp fires, and an occasional arrow point.

The Indian Well site, Fig. 10, No. 6, was discovered when someone disturbed part of it, the strong winds whipped away the fine sand and a few small beads were found. When excavations were stopped by rising waters thousands of them had been recovered, but except for stone rings, very little else. This site was about the center of the Long Narrows on the talus slope of a low cliff. It was probably a very ancient burying ground, although no

Fig. 14

STONE RING PENDANT, INDIAN WELL SITE

structure was apparent. Movement of the soil down the slope had thoroughly mixed it so the beads were evenly scattered. All were small, averaging 14 to the inch. Some diggers recovered 35,000 apiece. The few arrow points recovered were extremely crude. A few large sand-

Fig. 15

NOSTRIL PIPE, INDIAN WELL SITE

stone and scorious lava tube pipes were found, and one unusual type shown in Fig. 15, found by Frank Buehler at a depth of five feet. It is six and three-quarters of an inch long and two and one-eighth wide. The stem has two holes bored at an angle to meet the bowl at a depth of one and a half inches. This type of pipe was held to the nostrils to inhale the smoke, and is similar to ones found in the Southwest.

At the bottom of the talus slope, at a depth of about eight feet, a layer of yellow, water-deposited silt was uncovered, and in it were found beautifully worked willow leaf points. They resemble those found in the deepest and oldest part of the Five Mile Lock site; it is possible that they are 8000 or more years old. The structure of the deposit was also similar to the Five Mile Lock site, and completely different from the weathered talus above, in which the beads were found. The silt was laid down before the Long Narrows was cut. The talus was the result of centuries of weathering. The rising waters behind The Dalles Dam prevented an extensive investigation of this ancient site; it is now under 20 feet of water.

The Congdon and Maybe sites were similar as far as artifacts were concerned. Both had many knives and large stone beads, stone carvings, and atlatl weights; no atlatls were found in Indian Well. The large stone pipes, Fig. 48, came from both although not in quantity. Stone rings were also found, as they were in Indian Wells. Both sites were ancient burial grounds superimposed on still more ancient campsites. Amateurs believe these villages were there before the Long Narrows was formed, when

Fig. 16

DIGGING IN THE INDIAN WELL SITE

the river was a wide rapid reaching to the edge of the present railroad track.

The Five Mile Site, WS-4, and No. 13 in Fig. 10, extended from the waters edge at the start of the Long Narrows to the foot of the cliffs on the hillsides above. Between two basalt dikes beside the river a midden eleven feet deep had been built up, paralleling Wakemap in stratification and artifacts, although not enough scientific digging was done to establish any relationship. Evidence of cedar slabs and posts indicated the semi-subterranean type house, and the many arrow points suggested a hunting and fishing economy, with the latter probably the most important. Directly opposite this place was the narrowest part of the Long Narrows, and the most turbulent water. As shown in Fig. 10 , the wide expanse of the river suddenly contracts and the currents sweeping in from both sides of the obstruction generated violent whirlpools.

At the base of the cliff was a fairly level sand plain, with burials and cremations superimposed on an ancient campground. In the summer of 1952 and 1953 a crew under the direction of Dr. L. S. Cressman of the University of Oregon excavated six pits in this area; in some

Fig. 17

STONE SCULPTURE, CONGDON SITE

(Morton collection)

artifacts were heavily concentrated, others were sterile. A layer of artifact bearing hardpan was uncovered, and an outcropping of the same stratum discovered in the nearby highway cut, so work was transferred to this more accessible place as the loose structure of the midden itself, away from the hardpan, made deep pits unsafe to work in. This new digging was called the Roadcut Site of WS-4.

Over a period of two years Dr. Cressman's crew sank their excavations nearly 30 feet through layer after layer of occupational debris. The lowest stratum was a silty clay, partially water deposited, laid down near the end of the ice age when the river carried a larger volume of water than it does now, and had not yet cut its deep

Fig. 18

(Photo courtesy Dr. L. S. Cressman)
WS-4, ROADCUT SITE ON THE LONG NARROWS
Over 10,000 years of continuous occupation.

channel. This was the start of the early period of the site, dated by the "carbon 14" method as 9,785 years ago. Since this was a composite date for the layer, the bottom may have been as much as 11,000 years old. Artifacts were limited below level 33, a few bone specimens and some scrapers and blades. Stone implements were made by percussion flaking; pressure flaking was not used even for retouching. Between level 32 and 25 artifacts increased in number; besides bolas, blades and burins, there were large numbers of salmon vertebrae and bird and animal bones. Some of the bones were of animals now extinct, such as a vulture, and bones of the Condor which is now found only in California. Attention was being paid to personal appearance and decoration since red ochre paint was found in various stages of preparation. Birds, which were probably numerous in the nearby backwaters and pools, were captured with the bola, an instrument formed by tying weights to a series of strings which when thrown would entangle and trap the prey. Bone and antler artifacts were found, and stone projectile points, mostly non-stemmed. In the final part of the early period the bone and antler artifacts disappeared entirely, and there were no more bird or animal bones; occupation was sparse. The early period ended about 8,000 years ago.

In this final part of the early period atlatl hooks or spurs were found, one at level 28 and one at level 22. These were made of bone, with a base flattened for attachment to the atlatl, and a projecting point for engaging the base of the dart. These spurs are, I believe, the first definite evidence of the use of the atlatl on the Columbia. There have been many stone artifacts called "atlatl weights" found, but as yet there is no proof that they were actually used for this purpose.

For the next 2,000 years, occupation of the site was light. Cobble choppers commenced to replace blades as tools, the projectile points were few, there were no bolas, burins, or antler or bone artifacts.

The later period, from about 6,000 years ago until recently, commenced at level 10 and was marked by an increase in occupation, a decrease and disappearance of cobble choppers and non-stemmed points, and an increase in scrapers, gravers, and punches. Many different types of stemmed points appear. In the later stages of the late period, steatite beads and carved pendants, carved pestles and mauls and the first stone bowls appear. The appearance of trade articles marked the end of the period and the coming of the white man.

In this site at Five Mile Rapids native man had lived continuously for approximately 10,000 years, one of the oldest continuously occupied sites in America. Its residents were a river people, existing on the bounty of the Columbia, for they were not primarily hunters. During the time this site was occupied the weather and environment had changed drastically. In the early period the weather was about as now, mild and moist; food was plentiful and the population increased. Gradually it got drier and warmer, building up to a great altithermal, that is, a dry hot period, which started about 7,500 years ago and lasted about 3,500 years (authorities do not agree on the date of the altithermal). Food was scarce during this time and existence was a struggle; population decreased. In the Great Basin to the Southeast the lakes and marshes dried up and the people were forced to move. Possibly it was at this time that they followed the passes over the mountains and occupied the valleys and the coast. Some, certainly, sought out the Columbia where existence, though hard, was at least possible. It is reasonable to assume that WS-4 was but one of many other places on the Columbia that was occupied by relatively small groups engaged in catching fish and probably everything that swam, ran, flew, or crawled.

As the weather moderated and gradually returned to a moist temperate climate, the environment improved and living rose above the subsistence level. The population increased notably and development was rapid, culminating in the high culture that was responsible for the many examples of primitive art in the Columbia River valley.

But the early residents of WS-4 were not the first to occupy the valley. Sometime before about 11,000 years ago there were a primitive stone age people subsisting as best they could along the river, unaware of the terrible fate in store for them. This was about the end of the Pleistocene; the long tenacles of the ice age that had gripped the land, freezing out all life, were retreating, and the Columbia carried immense quantities of water from the melting glaciers. The weather was mild and moist, about like that which we presently enjoy.

Near the Idaho-Montana border a remnant of the ice age extended southward, forming a huge dam behind which collected a lake; at Missoula, Montana, the waters were nearly a thousand feet deep. All the valleys of Montana were filled, and mountain peaks rose above the waters as islands. Gradually, as the weather moderated, the dam grew weaker until one day part of it failed, the rushing waters hastened the total collapse, and what may have been the most spectacular, the most gigantic flood ever to occur in the New World was born. In one titanic rush 500 cubic miles of water was on its way to the sea, more water than the Columbia usually discharges in ten years. Across the Idaho Panhandle and into Washington near Spokane poured the wall of water, thence southeasterly toward Wallula Gap. Past Spokane the flood gouged out basins that are now lakes, and stripped the soil down to bedrock in a path that is sometimes 75 miles wide, the famous Channeled Scablands of Eastern Washington. Wallula Gap, running full, failed to carry the flood, and it spilled over the hills and cut a series of channels. The water backed up and flooded the Walla Walla valley. Down the Columbia poured the flood hundreds of feet deep, crushing all life before it; none that lived in the valley could escape.

Great banks of gravel were deposited where the current was turned by the hills, and in one of these banks near the John Day River that was being excavated for road material, hundreds of feet above the present Columbia, Dr. Cressman found a crude blade cemented in the gravel matrix. It had been picked up by the flood and tumbled along with the rocks, smoothing its surface. During excavations at The Dalles Dam, Sam Sargent, resident geologist, found in sand underneath a layer of the Spokane flood gravels some charcoal remains and worked stone tools. In the Roadcut site were found cobble choppers that had been water-worn after being first made, then re-sharpened. These may have been made before the flood and found by later residents, who by a bit of sharpening had a serviceable chopper. Very little will ever be known about these people; their campsites and villages were swept away by the flood, and all we have is evidence that they were here a long time ago.

Near the outlet of the Celilo Canal, at the lower end of the Long Narrows, was a village site that covered approximately ten acres. Much disturbed by highway, canal, and railroad construction, the original limits could not be determined, and of course, now it is all under water. This was supposed to be the original Wasco village, and a great many artifacts were recovered from it during the various activities. At the Oregon Historical Society Library is an old picture taken during the grading of a wagon road through the area, and each side of the cut is strewn with broken bowls, pestles, and other artifacts.

Excavations in this site revealed no information on house types. It may be that this village was occupied only during the fishing season—if so, the houses would have been temporary and built of mats and poles. It is known that the Tenino, neighbors of the Wasco, had their villages away from the river. Extensive excavations by amateurs along the lower edge of the site, near the river, uncovered a great many beautiful arrow points, but very little else. In any case, the site was extensively used, and for a long time.

THE LONG NARROWS TO THE SNAKE RIVER

Four miles above the Long Narrows was Brown's Island, also known as Rabbit Island, which was a peninsula except in high water. Between this island and the main Oregon shore was one of the narrowest places on the river, called the Short Narrows or Ten Mile Rapids. Lt. Clark says, "At 9 oClock a.m. I Set out with the party and proceeded on down a rapid stream of about 400 yards

wide. at 2½ miles the river widened into a large bason to
the Stard. Side on which there is five Lodges of Indians.
here a tremendious black rock Presented itself (Brown's
Island) high and Steep appearing to choke up the river;
nor could I see where the water passed further than the
current was drawn with great velocity to the Lard. Side of
this rock at which place I heard a great roreing. I landed
at the lodges and the natives went with me to the top of
this rock which makes from the Stard. Side, from the top
of which I could see the dificueltis we had to pass for
Several miles below; at this place the water of this great
river is compressed into a chanel between two rocks not
exceeding foty five yards wide and continues for ¼ of
a mile when it again widens to 200 yards and continues
this width for about 2 miles when it is again intersepted
by rocks (Upper Memaloose Island). This obstruction in
the river accounts for the water in high floods riseing to
Such a hite at the last falls (Celilo). The whole of the
Current of this great river must at all stages pass thro'
this narrow channel of 45 yards wide. as the portage of
our canoes over this high rock would be impossible with
our Strength and the only danger in passing thro those
narrows was the whorls and swills arriseing from the
Compression of the water, and which I thought as also
our principal waterman Peter Crusat by good stearing we
could pass down safe, accordingly I deturmined to pass
through this place notwithstanding the horrid appearance
of this agitated gut swelling, boiling & whorling in every
direction, which from the top of the rock did not appear
as bad as when I was in it; however we passed Safe to the
astonishment of all the Inds. of the last Lodges who
viewed us from the top of the rocks." I have gone through
these rapids in a 14 foot boat without much difficulty.
But for the long narrow hollowed out logs, heavily loaded,
used by Lewis and Clark, the large boils and whirlpools
that suddenly burst to the surface from the velocity of
the current would have made it a difficult passage. It was,
of course, completely impassable in high water.

Despite the heavy occupancy evident at this excellent fishery, very few artifacts were ever found there. Mr. Brown, owner of the Island and a most interesting character, had lived there for years; all he ever found was a few pestles. There were, however, many petroglyphs on the cliffs. Near the center of the island on the flat water-washed bedrock were several of them; carvings on a horizontal surface are rare. On a boulder near the upper end of the Island was a picture of a hunter with a bow and arrow and an excellent representation of an antelope. The relativery quiet waters between the Island and Celio Falls, about three miles above, was a famous place for taking salmon with nets; the shore was once covered with banded net sinkers.

Celilo Falls was the most spectacular and best known of all the fishing spots on the Columbia in modern times. Because it was visible from the highway, thousands of tourists stopped there to watch the Indians fish, which

Fig. 19

(Seufert collection, Oregon Historical Society)
FISHING AT CELILO FALLS, ABOUT 1898
The structure in the background is a causeway to reach an island.

they could do irrespective of controls applicable to white fishermen. The treaty of 1855, by which several tribes gave up their lands, permitted them to fish at their accustomed places for all time.

Here was a sight worth going miles to see. Over the raging torrent from every vantage point projected flimsy plank platforms from which the Indians plied their nets, four or five feet in diameter and with 20 foot handles, sweeping the waters downstream to trap the salmon, fighting their way through the violent waters. Many of the fishermen were lost before custom required each to be secured with a safety rope about the waist, as no man could live in those waters, and a fighting 50 pound salmon is hard to control on a slippery platform. Cableways provided access to the rocks in midstream, and channels were blasted to improve fishing. About it all clustered a picturesque Indian village of shacks built of rough boards and packing boxes, with Indian women in moccasins and beaded dresses, and with shiny new Buicks and Chevrolets in the dusty yards. Fortunate are those who spent a day here absorbing the vivid scene, for the like will never be seen again.

In prehistoric times the main village was on the Washington side of the river, now occupied by the railroad division point and town of Wishram, named after the old Indian village ten miles downstream at the Long Narrows. No sign is left of it now except the many burials among the steep rocks above the town. There was once also a village site on the Oregon side, but it does not appear to have been as large as the one opposite, and probably both were occupied only during the fishing season, which was short as the falls were drowned out during much of the best Chinook run. The Big Leap site was a burial ground upstream from the village on the Oregon side. From it were taken a great many chipped knives and arrow points, carved stone bowls, and ornaments. The site was so old that there was no sign of the burials and the Indians themselves were occasionally observed digging there for arrow points. What is not now flooded is being rapidly eroded away by the wind whipped waters of Lake Celilo behind The Dalles Dam, which cover the falls and all this historic and romantic region.

Miller Island, four miles upstream from Celilo, was once a most interesting place to visit. At this time a large portion of it is cultivated, and it is all used as a cattle range. On the southwest shoulder was a village site with 132 house pits, now leveled for a pasture. Some of the pits were four or more feet deep, and artifacts were continually washing out of the river bank nearby. The entire island showed signs of occupancy, and there was a midden on the upper end and another about midway of the island on the Washington side. The latter washed out after the dam was filled, and a great quantity of beautiful agate spalls were uncovered, and some fine arrow points. The polished stone scrapers (Fig. 76) were found throughout the island, a dozen could be picked up in an afternoon. On the upper end overlooking the Oregon shore are rock shelters with red petroglyphs (and rattlesnakes). These shelters were excavated by the University of California in 1926.

The John Day bar sprawls opposite the mouth of the John Day River, and adjacent to the John Day Rapids, a region of swift water and "crouded with islands of bad rocks difficult & crooked passage". On the cliffs above the bar, which is about two miles long, are a number of especially fine petroglyphs and pictographs. The upper end was an occupied area now largely washed awey, and near the lower end is a deep midden with a disturbed burial site nearby. Part of the midden was eroded in the 1894 flood, leaving several inches of rock mixed with artifacts, commercial diggers cleaned it out years ago. The midden is rich in the finest of arrow points, but little else except notched sinkers. This bar, although difficult to reach, was heavily occupied, for the rapids made an excellent fishing spot. The John Day Dam will be built just below the lower end of it.

On the Oregon side at the mouth of the John Day there was a large village, through which both the railroad and highway are cut. It is reported that when the highway was graded several carved bowls were uncovered, and thrown back into the fill. Mr. and Mrs. Harrison, who live on the upper edge of the site, have uncovered a number of especialy fine artifacts, some of which are illustrated in this book (Figs. 39, 40, 41, 52, 68). There were a number of petroglyphs on a short cliff just below the mouth of the river, but they have all been chipped away by collectors.

About fourteen miles above the John Day's mouth, is Fountain Bar, which next to the Long Narrows, may have been the most heavily occupied area on the upper river. This bar is about two miles long and a large portion of it has been blown out; collectors have been picking up relics there for fifty years. At the lower end is Rock Creek, and the upper end is opposite the modern community of Blalock. The explorers, Lewis and Clark, stopped here on April 23, 1806, and camped with the Indians. "we continued our march along a narrow rocky bottom on the N. side of the river about 12 miles to Wah-how-pum Village of 12 temporary mat lodges near the Rock rapid. these people appeared much pleased to see us, sold us 4 dogs and some wood for our small articles which we had previously prepared as our only recourse to obtain fuel and food through plains. these articles consisted of pewter buttons, strips of tin iron and brass, twisted wire &c. we also obtained some shap-pe-lell (roots) newly made from these people. at a little distance below this village we passed five lodges of the same people who like those were waiting the arrival of the salmon. after we had arranged our camp we caused all the old and brave men to set arround and smoke with us." Their camp was just above Rock Creek. Here can still be seen a fish lead constructed of stones, to guide the salmon to a low cliff where they could be easily netted. It was useful only in high water.

Near the center of the bar there were several graves, now blown out, and there are a great number of others scattered about in the sand blows. The upper end of the bar has been washing away for years; the gravel left contains many arrow points, but they are all badly shattered from the action of the waves. In some places in the deep blows the flint spalls lie a foot or more deep; many of them are of beautiful stone. There are a few very poor petroglyphs on a cliff near the center of the bar,but two miles above the upper end is one of the best groups along the river, although several of them have been knocked off and carried away.

Between Fountain Bar and Umatilla were a number of camping grounds, notably at Sundale, Roosevelt, Moonax, Alderdale, and Blalock Island. At Alderdale there are some petroglyphs on boulders below the old ferry landing. One of them appears to be a picture of the axe shown in Fig. 56. A great many artifacts have come from this section of the river. The banks are subject to both washing and wind erosion. Surface hunting was good, and there has been considerable screening of the washed gravel layers. The 1894 and 1948 floods washed out many of the old camps, leaving the artifacts down beneath the boulders.

At Roosevelt there was a group of petroglyphs, most of which have been recently removed for souvenirs. Charley Beckman, a commercial digger, worked the gravel on the bar near the ferry landing for years, also the one opposite at Arlington. This is a beautiful stretch of the river, just swift enough to be interesting and full of traces of early man. Rock hounds, too, congregate there to hunt agates and petrified wood in the volcanic ash layers that show up as white streaks on the hill sides. A good place to get a tan too.

Just above the McNary Dam was Umatilla Rapids, a stretch of swift water that made excellent fishing. Lewis and Clark called them Mussell Shell Rapids because of the heaps of fresh water mussel shells in the village sites. Joel Shiner excavated a midden near there for the Smithsonian Institution, that was overlain with volcanic ash that may have come from the final eruption of Mt. Mazama. At Berrian was a large cemetery and camp ground, excavated by Dr. Douglas Osborne and subject of a report that should be required reading for anyone interesed in the Columbia River. See the bibliography. The area around the mouth of the Walla Walla and Snake rivers was heavily occupied. Sacajawea Park at Pasco is built on a midden. Lewis and Clark stopped there for a couple of days, noting: "we halted above the point on the river Kimooenim (Snake) to smoke with the Indians who had collected there in great numbers to view us". The Sacajawea Museum has an outstanding display of artifacts collected along this section of the river. Before McNary Dam was built, the small islands which occur every few miles along the river produced many artifacts as they were favorite camping grounds.

SNAKE RIVER TO THE BORDER

From the outlet of the Snake River to Kettle Falls, the Columbia flows through a dead land, hidden in its own rocky channel, cut through the basalt. Millions of years ago the river flowed south to the Pacific, but giant cracks opened up in the earth and from them welled flows of molten rock that spread over the land. Some of these flows were thousands of years apart, some hundreds of thousands, and rich soil was formed from the volcanic debris that supported forests and strange animals. New flows buried the forests, some of the trees were opalized and the source of the famous petrified wood gem stones of the Columbia. In Ginko State Park, at Vantage, Washington, many of these ancient trees are exposed, and in a museum in the park there is a marvelous display of petrified wood from different varieties of trees.

Successive flows of lava eventually piled up layer on layer until much of Eastern Washington was covered a mile and half deep. The Columbia was forced to swing far to the North against the granite hills and the lava plateau, now a rich farming area, became known as the Big

Bend country. Through the basalt the river cut a deep channel, much of it with vertical walls hundreds of feet high. Later, glaciers of the ice age dammed the channel and the river again flowed to the south, cutting the spectacular Moses and Grand Coulees. When the ice dam melted, the river returned to its old bed and left the famous Dry Falls, once the largest waterfall in the world. The coulee above Dry Falls is again full of water; it is used as a reservoir to store water pumped into it from the Columbia with power from Grand Coulee Dam, to be fed into a system of canals that is irrigating and transforming the desert into a rich garden.

Village sites dot the shores of the river between Pasco and Wenatchee. The Hanford project has closed the river from Richland to the Priest Rapids. I have never seen that part of the river. Before Hanford existed, large collections of artifacts were made from the old camps at the mouth of the Yakima, on both sides of the river at White Bluffs, and at Wahluke, and from the numerous small sites between. At Vernita just below Priest Rapids, was one of the largest sites, known as Yaeger Island, although it was an island only during high water. It was famous for beautiful, long barbed gem points. The 1894 and 1948 floods washed away most of it, uncovering a great many relics. Collectors have worked there for years.

Priest Rapids was named by the Astorian, Alexander Ross in 1811. "Soon after passing the Eyakema, a long range of marl hills (White Bluffs) interrupts the view on the east side of the river. Here two dead children were presented to us by their parents, in order that we might restore them to life again, and a horse was offered us as a reward. We pitied their ignorance, made them a small present, and told them to bury their dead. As we advanced along the marl hills, the river inclined gradually to the Northwest. After a good day's work, we stopped for the night near a small camp of Indians, who were very friendly to us. Here and there were to be seen, on small eminences, burial-places. The dead are interred, and a few small sticks always point out the cemetery.

"On the eighteenth we reached the end of the marl hills. Just at this place the river makes a bend right south for about ten miles, when a high and rugged hill confines it on our left. Here the increasing rapidity of the current gave us intimation that we were not far from some obstruction ahead, and as we advanced a little under the brow of the hill, a strong and rocky rapid presented itself in the very bend of the river. Having ascended it about half way, we encamped for the night.

"Here a large concourse of Indians met us, and after several friendly harangues, commenced the usual ceremony of smoking the pipe of peace, after which they passed the night in dancing and singing. The person who stood foremost in all these introductory ceremonies was a tall, meager, middle-aged Indian, who attached himself very closely to us from the first moment we saw him. He was called Haqui-laugh, which signifies doctor, or rather priest; and as this personage will be frequently mentioned in the sequel of our narrative, we have been thus particular in describing him. We named the place Priest's Rapids, after him."

The Priest Rapids area is one of the most rugged on the Columbia. From Vantage to the foot of the rapids is 28 miles, the first of the seven rapids starts 14 miles below Vantage and the others follow at intervals, separated by stretches of calm flowing water. The river drops 80 feet in this distance. The lower rapid was the worst of all; the river was divided into a series of boiling channels. One of them was called the Whale Chute, and down it the water rushed at great speed. Near the last rapid was the Sacred Island, consisting of solid rock and boulders on which there were at least 150 petroglyphs, carved in unusual designs. Several were removed by the Grant County Public Utility District, builders of the Priest Rapids Dam. Here were the last of the mat lodges of the Columbia River Indians, and the last dugout canoe used on the river, now preserved in a museum at Vantage.

Between Vantage and Priest Rapids every bar was used at one time or another for fishing camps, for the salmon was the main food of the Indians of the Upper Columbia as well as those below, and they passed here in prodigious numbers to the spawning grounds on the headwaters of the river. Above the mouth of the Snake, Lt. Clark says, "I took two men in a Small canoe and assended the Columbia river 10 miles to an Island near the Stard Shore on which two large Mat Lodges of Indians were drying Salmon, (as they informed me by Signs for the purpose of food and fuel, & I do not think it at all improbable that those people make use of Dried fish as fuel). The number of dead Salmon on the Shores & floating in the river is incrediable to say—and at this Season they have only to collect the fish Split them open and dry them on their Scaffolds of which they have great

Fig. 20

PETROGLYPHS NEAR VANTAGE

numbers". As the river cuts away the banks in its constant wanderings, and as the floods run over the bars, the sand is carried away, leaving the artifacts on the beach among the rocks, to be again covered with the shifting sands. Collectors have worked this section of the river for years, throwing off the blow sand and screening the layer of rocks below. The number of arrow points collected is astounding, and some of the finest on the river are found here.

Between Vantage and Trinidad is one of the few parts of the river still accessible only by boat, but it has been well explored and extensively hunted. Upstream from Vantage Bridge are several groups of petroglyphs, one of which can be reached by a trail made for that purpose and exhibits the characteristic traits of the American sightseer, being practically obliterated by painted and pecked initials and names, and covered by a generous application of white and colored chalk. Those that take a little effort to reach are still pristine, however, and well worth the trouble to see.

About four miles above the bridge is a creek called Whiskey Dick, named after an early settler with obvious habits, at the outlet of this creek is a large bar that shows evidence of heavy occupancy. Several graves have washed out in past years, and occupants of the isolated ranch here have made collections from the beach. At Quillomene Rapids, about 12 miles above the bridge, is a large site on either side of the river. The one on the west side is covered with a large sand dune, the beach has been heavily worked for arrow points. There are several house pits on the bar opposite. Above Quillomene Creek is a looted graveyard covering the surface of a low mound. Here starts Osborne Bar, extending five or six miles upstream, with indications of house pits in several places. About eight miles below Trinidad is Churchyard Bar; on the bench above was a cemetery called Simmon's Graveyard after its discoverer. From it were taken a number of carved mauls, pipes and ornaments. On the west side of the river is a vertical cliff rising from the waters edge several hundred feet. In the center of it is standing, as if it grew there, a petrified tree. It is said that Crescent and West Bars, near Trinidad, were worked by eastern universities during the early part of the present century, and large collections made.

I have not hunted the river above Trinidad. There were sites at the entrances of all the small rivers above Wenatchee, but this area was not as heavily occupied as the river below. An extensive survey of the Chief Joseph Reservoir, between Bridgeport and Grand Coulee Dam, was made by Dr. Osborne, Robert Crabtree and Alan Bryan, and reported in *American Antiquity*, April, 1952. Sixteen sites were investigated, none of which indicated extensive occupancy.

Above Grand Coulee Dam there were fishing sites in several places. These were investigated and reported on in *"Archaeology of the Upper Columbia Region,"* by David Collier, Alfred Hudson and Arlo Ford. They found that the population had been sparse, and closely affiliated with the Fraser and Thompson river regions. In 150 miles, and 14 months work, they located only 35 definite sites, some of which were excavated. They contrast this area with that of the Long Narrows, where Strong, Schenck and Steward in 1926 located 22 sites in 15 miles; and since then more have been found.

Kettle Falls was about 40 miles south of the Canadian border, a series of rapids and falls where the Indians living in the Colville country took their salmon. "The Indian village is situated about two miles below the fort," wrote Paul Kane, "on a rocky eminence overlooking the Kettle Falls. These are the highest in the Columbia River. They are about one thousand yards across, and eighteen feet high. The immense body of water tumbling amongst the broken rocks renders them exceedingly picturesque and grand. The Indians have no particular name for them, giving them the general name of Tumtum, which is applied to all falls of water. The voyageurs call them the "Chaudiere," or Kettle Falls, from the numerous round holes worn in the solid rocks by loose boulders. These boulders, being caught in the inequalities of rocks below the falls, are constantly driven round by the tremendous force of the current, and wear out holes as perfectly round and smooth as in the inner surface of a cast-iron kettle. The village has a population of about 500 souls, called, in their own language, Chualpays. They differ but little from the Walla-Wallas. The lodges are formed of mats of rushes stretched on poles. A flooring is made of sticks, raised three or four feet from the ground, leaving the space beneath it entirely open, and forming a cool, airy, and shady place, in which their salmon are hung to dry."

Fort Colville was established near Kettle Falls in 1826 by the Hudson's Bay Company. All is now under many feet of water of Roosevelt Lake behind Grand Coulee Dam.

BURIAL SITES

The tribes west of the Cascades did not bury their dead until very recent times, instead the bodies were wrapped in robes or mats and deposited in canoes in the woods or on a rocky point or island, or in vaults made of cedar boards or split canoes, or simply placed in trees. No prehistoric burial grounds have ever been found on the lower Columbia. Skeleton remains are occasionally seen protruding from the banks in old village sites but they are the remains of Indians who lay where they died in the great pestilence of the 1830s and were covered with flood silt.

Many of these places of deposit are known. Most famous are Mt. Coffin, Coffin Rock, Warrior Rock, Cascades, Upper and Lower Memaloose Island, and Blalock Island. Mt Coffin was a large rock near the mouth of the Cowlitz River. Franchére says: "We passed a large village on the south bank, called Kreluit, above which is a fine forest of oaks; and encamped for the night; on a low point, at the foot of an isolated rock, about one hundred and fifty feet high. This rock appeared to me remarkable on account of its situation, reposing in the midst of a low and swampy ground, as if it had been dropped from the clouds, and seeming to have no connection with the neighboring mountains. On a cornice or shelving projection about thirty feet from its base, the natives of the adjacent villages deposit their dead, in canoes; it is the same rock to which, for this reason, Lieutenant Broughton gave the name of Mt. Coffin." In 1841 Lt. Charles Wilkes,

Fig. 21

(Seufert collection, Oregon Historical Society)
VAULT BURIAL, GRAVE ISLAND NEAR THE DALLES, OREGON

U. S. Army, camped nearby, allowed a fire to escape and burned a number of the canoes, to the great anger of the natives. The rock has now been quarried away for road building material.

Coffin Rock is a small island opposite the mouth of the Kalama River. It was once covered with canoes as was the rocky point on the main shore. Alexander Henry says, "We soon came to a large village at the entrance of a small river (Kalama) on the N. A long range of houses runs parallel with the river, and the natives appear numerous. Opposite this village, on the S., is a point of rocks on which their dead are deposited in wooden canoes; and immediately above this point is a rock island, on the top of which are also dead bodies in canoes—one apparently that of a great chief, from the manner in which he is arranged. The Island is called Coffin Rock." A reporter for the Portland *Oregonian* called attention to the island in 1880 " . . . as so few relics exist of the past race. In this connection Coffin Rock further down the river is worthy of note as it was at one time crowded with the dead, and has probably been the depository for ages. As it was customary to leave not only the implements of the chase but the ornaments and articles of general use, a skillful and intelligent search might reveal something of interest. It is thought by some that the disposition of fine canoes and other valuables was not so much with a view to any use in the future but rather to prevent quarrels among the living for the property left."

Warrior Rock is at the lower tip of Sauvies Island. There is no sign whatever left of the thousands of bodies which once covered these landmarks.

At the Cascades, on a spot now occupied by the Fort Rains Inn at North Bonneville, was a vault burial site seen and described by several early writers, as it was near the portage path. The Rev. Samuel Parker writes, "As I continued down the Indian path, at no great distance from the village, I came to several depositories of the dead. They were built of planks split from balsam fir and cedar, about eight feet long, six wide, and five high, and well covered. At one end is what might be called a door, upon which were paintings of various devices, which did not appear to be designed for any other purpose than for ornamentation. Some had paintings on the sides as well as the doors. The number of these depositories I did not ascertain, as many of them were far decayed, as hardly to be distinguishable; but of those in good condition there were eight or ten." Railroad and highway construction has destroyed this site, but buttons and beads can still be found between the railroad track and the river where fill material was deposited while grading for the railroad.

A small island called Sullivan Island, just above the Cascades, was also used as a vault burial site. Don Gallagher of Stevenson told me that "The captain of one of the tug boats here said his grandmother visited the

Fig. 22

UPPER MEMALOOSE ISLAND, 1956
The three houses were used for depositing the dead.

Island about 1850; she said there were three shacks built of split cedar planks, with bodies laying on shelves and on the floor. The whites burned the place about 1855 because it smelled so bad." There were a few modern graves there which were removed and the remains reburied near North Bonneville when the dam was built. This island, now nearly washed away, has been thoroughly dug over; stone material was scarce but many buttons and other trade goods, badly burnt, were found. There were also burials on Bradford Island, now part of Bonneville Dam.

The most famous of the vault burial islands was Lower Memaloose, just below Lyle, Washington. It was used by the Indians of The Dalles. Lewis and Clark named it Sepulchre Island when they stopped there on April 13, 1806. "We halted a fiew minits at the Sepulchar rock and examined the deposit of the dead at that place. Those were constructed in the same manner of those already described below the rapids. Some of them were more than half filled with dead bodies. there was 13 sepulchers on this rock which stands near the center of the river, and has a surface of about two acres above the water." This place was not used after about 1880. The monument on the southeast shoulder that can be seen from the highway marks the grave of Victor Trevett, early pioneer who died in 1883; his will specified that he be buried on the island "with his friends the Indians." The island was robbed for years until all the remains were removed when Bonneville Dam was built. Early in this century someone collected a number of bones for ship-

Fig. 23

(Photo courtesy Mrs. W. A. Husbands)
LOWER MEMALOOSE ISLAND, 1894

ment to some unknown destination. The station agent, at a loss as to how to bill the shipment, finally recorded: "One Chinook, knocked down". It was stopped at The

Dalles, and the shipper forced to replace the bones on the island.

The Upper Memaloose Island, Fig. 22, was set aside by act of Congress as a burial ground for the exclusive use of the Yakima Indians, and it was a federal offense for white people to go there, although that did not stop many. It was in use until 1956, when the remains of about 2500 Indians were removed by helicopter and reburied near the Washington end of The Dalles Bridge.

On the upstream end of Blalock Island were several vaults. Little is left of them now. Lewis and Clark stopped there, again noting in their Journals: "on the upper part of this Island wee discovered an Indian Vault, our curiosity induced us to examine the method those nativs practiced deposeing the dead, the vault was made of broad boads and pieces of Canoes leaning on a ridge pole which was Suported by 2 forks Set in ground six feet in hight in an easterly and westerly direction about 60 feet in length, and 12 feet wide, in it I observed great numbers of homane bones of every description perticularly in a pile near the center of the vault, on the East end 21 scul bomes forming a circle on Mats; in the westerly part of the Vault appeared to be appropriated for those of more recent death, as many of the bodies of the deceased raped up on leather robes lay on boards covered with mats, &c. we observed independent of the canoes which served as a covering, fishing nets of various kinds, Baskets of different sizes, wooden boles, robes Skins, trenchers, and various kind of trinkets, in and suspended on the ends of the pieces forming the vault; we also Saw the Skeletons of Several Horses at the vault a great number of bones about it, which convinced me that those animals were Sacrefised as well as the above articles to the Deceased." Vault burial was also practiced along the Snake River.

It is from these old burial vault sites that most of the trade goods are collected. All traces of the vaults and remains have disappeared long ago, but the buttons and beads are still scattered throughout the soil. In some, after the wind has blown away the fine sand, the beads lay in a multi-colored film, shimmering in the sun. Rolled copper beads are found by the hundreds, and occasionally one of the historic Phoenix or Colonial buttons is uncovered by the shifting sands. The practice of vault burial must be fairly modern because stone work is seldom found in them. How the hundreds of thousands who died along the lower river in prehistoric times were interred is still a mystery.

Cremation was practiced by some tribes and cremation pits, rock encircled basins in which the funeral pyre was built, are found from the vicinity of The Dalles to about Priest Rapids. There is considerable evidence to show that the bodies were exposed in sheds until entirely decomposed before cremating. The scarcity of wood and the very real fear of being burned alive would have discouraged cremation immediately after death.

The practice of exposure and later cremation is a comparatively recent cultural trait that lasted into historical times. While a few of the cremations are entirely lacking in trade goods, showing prehistoric origin, most of them do contain buttons and beads, and in a few there are no stone age implements whatever except a few arrow points. Beneath some of the cremations there are burials, indicating a transition from interment to cremation by the same culture. Cremation pits are always rich in artifacts and have been diligently sought for by amateurs. Most of them were haphazardly excavated long ago, as they were well marked and easily found.

There is considerable evidence to show that some type of cremation was practiced far back in the stone age. At the Indian Well, Big Leap, Maybe, and Atlatl Valley sites evidence of burning was uncovered. Due to the age of the sites and the shifting talus slopes, evidence was superficial at Indian Well. None of the artifacts were burned, but bits of calcined bone were found, and occasionally a streak of burned earth and charcoal. The stone rings shown in Fig. 14 and 46, along with two others, were found close to one of the areas showing evidence of fire. Two of the stone pipes in Fig. 48 were found in the Maybe site on the edge of a small burned area containing pieces of charred bone. On Miller Island a blown out grave was found containing parts of a charred skeleton, the parts not altered by fire had disappeared long ago. A basalt knife and chert spear point were found in it. These types indicate a ceremonial burning of the possessions of the deceased near the body, rather than cremation of the remains because the bones are merely partially charred or discolored by the fire, and no attempt was made to consume them. Traces of discoloration of the sand, or bits of skeletal material in some instances, show that these were true burials.

In Atlatl Valley and the Maybe site a few small bundles of burned material were found, the evidence indicated that these remains were cremated elsewhere and buried in a small hole. The bundles consisted of charcoal, ashes, small bits of cremated bone, and occasionally an arrow point or flake of burned stone. In no case was there sufficient material to determine the origin, perhaps they were not human. There has been no scientific investigation of these ancient practices.

Graves which appear to be the oldest are merely pits dug two or three feet deep, the body flexed and placed in the pit and covered, and a mound of rocks placed on top. These are found in The Dalles and John Day areas with several feet of sand and earth over the cap rock. No skeletal material whatever remains, some may have a slightly darker shade to the sand but even this evidence is often lacking. Only the artifacts identify them as graves.

There are hundreds of burial grounds, cremation pits, and vault sites along the river, many of which have been excavated for the artifacts. There are probably a great many that have not been discovered. It is, of course, illegal and unethical to dig a grave.

HOUSES

Between the Long Narrows and the coast the Natives lived in houses constructed of planks split from cedar, with shed or hip roofs of either cedar bark or plank. Usually a pit was dug one to four feet deep, the wall planks set vertically to the eaves, a small hole left in one end for a door, and an opening left in the roof for the smoke to escape. The door was a plank suspended from a thong, and the planks about the smoke hole were loose so they could be moved to permit control of the opening. Several families occupied one house; planks were sometimes individually owned and considered a valuable piece

Fig. 24

CEDAR PLANK CARVING
Found floating in the Columbia by William Seufert during the 1894 flood.

of property. If an occupant moved, he could take his share of the house with him. Houses were about 20 feet wide and might be 40 or more feet long. Boards averaged two inches thick and two feet wide, although some having a width of five and a half feet have been recorded. They were split from the cedar trees with elkhorn wedges and stone hammers, then shaped with an adze and abrasive stones.

Alexander Henry gives a good description of a house located in the center of the present town of Cascade Locks " . . . We passed over to the Cathlayackty village on the S., which is situated in the woods, at some distance from the river. The chief, whose house we entered, was a portly old man, who looked more respectable than any other I had seen on the Columbia. He was very civil to us, and spread down near the fire a clean white biche-skin (elk skin) for us to sit on. The houses appeared in a state of confusion, everything having been removed but a few old wattap cooking utensils. These houses are sunk about three feet under the ground; the entrance is at one end by a narrow oval door, with a knotty log on the inside for a ladder. Next the door, and facing it is a plank partition, behind which is the fireplace, about 10 feet square, sunk two feet below the ground floor of the house. At the other end is another partition of planks, behind which a range of beds, raised three feet from the ground, occupies the furthermost end of the house and runs round on both sides to opposite the partition near the door. The front planks of the beds are carved and painted in various styles. At the end of each range are some broad upright planks, on which figures are rudely carved, somewhat resembling fluted pillars. At the foot of the chief's bed are planted in the ground at equal distances four figures of human heads, about two feet high, adorned with a kind of crown, and rudely painted. Beside these figures are erected in the ground two large, flat, painted stones. On the side of each partition, facing the fireplace, are carved and painted on the planks, uncouth figures of eagles, tortoises, and other animals, some of them four feet long. The colors are white, red, black, and green; the sculpture, in some instances, is not bad." The midden from the village in which this house stood can still be seen next to the Columbia Hotel, in Cascade Locks. N. G. Seaman, in his book *"Indian Relics of the Pacific Northwest,"* shows pictures of carved boards like those described by Henry.

After returning from his discovery exploration of the Willamette River, Lt. Clark stopped at the Ne-cha-co-kee village (MU 19) near the river's edge, on the western end of Blue Lake, below Troutdale. "at 3 P. M. we arived at the residence of our Pilot which consists of one long house with seven appartments or rooms in squar form about 30 feet. each room opening into a passage which is quite through the house. those passages are about 4

Fig. 25

REPLICA OF A CHINOOK PLANK HOUSE

feet in width and formed of wide boads set on end in the ground and reaching to the Ruff which serves also as divisions to the rooms. this house is built of bark of the white cedar Supported on long stiff poles resting on the ends of broad boads which form the rooms &c." Lt. Clark's sketch of this house shows that it was 226 feet long and 30 feet wide, divided with four passageways. Maj. O. S. McLeary, an early student of local history, says that in 1923 the marks of the house were still visible. Dikes and other construction have now obliterated the site.

Although constructed with great skill, such houses were not ideal protection from the elements. There were many cracks between the boards where the wind could penetrate, and the fit about the gables and eaves was not good. The roofs, too, leaked, and it was frequently necessary to erect skin shelters over the beds. These, however, were minor hardships to a people used to going naked and barefoot winter and summer, and unacquainted with creature comforts. If not destroyed by fire, an ever present menace, these cedar houses would last for several decades.

The houses of a village generally extended in a row along the river bank, sometimes close together and sometimes with a considerable distance in between them. On Lake River, where outlines of the houses can still be seen, they measure in one village 25 feet wide and 85, 120, 40, and 90 feet long, spaced 10 or 15 feet apart. Another site has one continuous house pit 300 feet long and 25 feet wide, although slight elevations across the pit indicate either passageways or separate houses. This was a fairly recent or short lived town, as the midden in the pit is only a foot or so deep. Wherever house pits are visible, there is always a small circular house pit to the rear and close by; the reason for this is not clear, but it is thought it was an isolation house for girls at puberty.

Villages were occupied only part of year, in the fishing season the entire population might move to a good site, carrying boards of their houses with them for erection into shelters with the assistance of mats; or they might have frames ready for erection of the boards in both places. Another reason for moving was the enormous number of fleas that would accumulate in the dwellings. These vermin were close to a national calamity for the natives, and white men always approached an Indian village with extreme caution. The Indians knew of no way to reduce their number or escape their savage attacks except to move when they became unbearable. Lewis and Clark state: "The flees are so noumerous in this countrey and difficult to get cleare of that the Indians have diff't. houses & villages to which they remove frequently to get rid of them, and not withstanding all their precautions, they never step into our hut without leaveing sworms of those troublesome insects. I scercely get to sleep half the night clear of the torments of those flees, with the precaution of haveing my blankets serched and the flees killed every day. The 1st of those insects we saw on the Columbia River was at the 1st Great Falls (Celilo)". Seargent Gass says about the village at the mouth of the Klickitat River "Passed a place where there was a village in good order when we went down; but has been lately torn down, and again erected a short distance from the old ground where it formerly stood. The reason for this removal I cannot conjecture, unless to avoid the fleas, which are more numerous in this country than any insects I ever saw."

Semi-subterranean houses were used prior to those made of plank, and were still used up until the beginning of the last century but mostly above the Long Narrows. Some near Bingen were described by Lewis and Clark: "Here I observed several habitations under ground; they were sunk about 8 feet deep and covered with strong timber and several feet of earth in a conic form. those habitations are avacuated at present. they are about 16 feet in diameter, nearly circular, and are entered through a hole at top which appears to answer the double purpose of a chimney and dore. from this enterance you descend to the flore by a ladder". A site near Camas (CL 16) has eleven of the pits left from this type of house, and one on Millers Island had 132, recently leveled for a pasture.

Lodges made of tule mats spread on a framework of poles were the most common type of habitation of the natives above the Long Narrows. They were easily moved and afforded sufficient shelter in the dry climate east of the Cascades. They too, were usually set in a shallow pit, these were found by the hundreds on the upper river but most of them have now disappeared beneath the waters.

There are several, however, between Roosevelt and the river that will be there until the John Day Dam is finished , although they are quite modern.

Fig. 26

(Photo by Click Relander)
MAT HOUSE AT PRIEST RAPIDS, 1950

Alexander Ross says about the Okanogan country Indians: "Their winter habitations are constructed chiefly of mats and poles, covered over with grass and earth, and made very commodious, comfortable, and roomy, the inside being dug about a foot or two below the surface of the ground, a precaution which adds much to their comfort. They are invariable open at the ridge pole all along, and the reason is obvious, for without any chimney, the smoke by this means has a free vent upwards. These lodgings resemble in appearance the roof of a common dwelling house removed from the walls and placed on the ground. The fires are made in the center directly under the ridge pole and about six feet apart, and are in proportion to the number of families who live under the same roof, each family having generally one fire. The doors are but few, and situated to suit convenience, in the front, back, or the gable ends; and are merely oblong holes, over which mats are suspended by means of a wooden hinge, which mat or door must be lifted up and down every time a person goes in or out." Mat lodges of this type were used up to the last few years, now they are all made of canvas.

Lewis and Clark describe the mat house thus: "The houses or Lodges of the tribes of the main Columbia river is of large mats made of rushes, those houses are from 15 to 60 feet in length generally of an Oblong squar form, supported by poles on forks in the inner side, Six feet high, the top is covered also with mats leaveing a Seperation in the whole length of about 12 or 15 inches wide, left for the purpose of admitting light and for the Smok of the fire to pass which is made in the middle of the house. The roughfs are nearly flat, which proves to me that the rains are not common in this open countrey. Those people appear of a mild disposition and friendly disposed. They have in their huts independent of their nets gigs & fishing tackling each bows and large quivers of arrows on which they use flint spikes."

The last mat houses on the Columbia were used by the Wanapums at Priest Rapids, one of them is shown in Fig. 26. It was still in use in 1952. The Wanapums had lived in this area since long before historic times, in 1800 they numbered about 2,500 but by 1958 they had shrunk to four members. Since they did not oppose the white invasion, they never were part of a treaty and so were not subject to the doles of the government. The Grant County Public Utility District, builders of the Priest Rapids Dam, provided for protection of their burial grounds and preserved some sacred carved rocks in the rapids. The District assisted remaining members of the tribe to re-settle outside of the area to be flooded, and employed archaeologists to explore the ancient campsites along the river behind the dam.

CANOES

The life of the Indians in prehistoric times along the Columbia was centered about their canoes. The advanced stage of the art of their construction, evident at the time of contact, indicates a long and progressive cultural trait. All of the early explorers were astonished at the grace and utility of native canoes, and the skill with which they were handled. Sergeant Ordway, with the Lewis and Clark expedition, said: "I must give these Savages as well as those on the coast the praise of makeing the neatest and handsomest lightest best formed canoes I ever saw & are the best hands to work them." With the canoe the Indians were masters of the river; travel, intercourse, and trade were possible with distant and different tribes.

Hayden Island, over which the Interstate Bridge between Vancouver and Portland passes, was named Image Canoe Island by Lewis and Clark, because of an exceptionally large and well-decorated canoe they saw emerging from behind it. "We proceeded on met a large and Small canoe from below with 12 men. the large canoe was ornimented with Images carved in wood the figures of a Bear in front & a man in stern, Painted & fixed verry netely on the canoe, rising to near the hight of a man." Sergeant Ordway also noticed the canoe and its inhabitants, "towards evening we met several Indians in a handsom canoe which had a Immage on the bow. one of the Indians could talk and Speak some words English Such as curseing and blackguard."

Canoes were always made of a single log of the red cedar. The tree was felled and cut to length with fire and stone and bone adze blades, and with the same tools the log was shaped and hollowed out. After being trimmed to the proper shape it was filled with water and by means of hot stones the water was boiled until the wood was softened, the sides were then stretched and bent to the proper form and held fast by thwarts sewn to the sides.

After drying, the canoe would hold its shape. The interior and exterior was then carefully sanded down with scorious lava, sandstone, and sharkskin. The abrasive stones used for the purpose are found all along the river. Bow and stern pieces were carved with stone adzes and beaver tooth chisels, then mortised into place and sewn on with spruce roots through holes drilled with stone drills. Afterwards the canoe was painted inside and out. James G. Swan in *"The Northwest Coast"* describes how an Indian Canoe was made:

Fig. 27

(Photo courtesy Mel-o's Camera Shop, The Dalles)

NATIVE DUGOUT CANOE ON THE COLUMBIA, ABOUT 1880

"The manufacture of a canoe is a work of great moment with these Indians. It is not every man among them that can make a canoe, but some are, like our white mechanics, more expert than their neighbors. A suitable tree is first selected, which in all cases is the cedar, and then cut down. This job was formerly a formidable one, as the tree was chipped around with stone chisels, after the fashion adopted by beavers, and looks as if gnawed off. At present, however, they understand the use of the axe, and many are expert choppers. When the tree is down, it is first stripped of its bark, then cut off into the desired length, and the upper part split off with little wedges, till it is reduced to about two thirds the original height of the log. The bow and stern are then chopped into a rough shape, and enough cut out of the inside to lighten it so that it can be easily turned. When all is ready, the log is turned bottom up, and the Indian goes to work to fashion it out. This he does with no instrument of measurement but his eye, and so correct is that, that when he has done his hewing no one could detect the least defect. When the outside is formed and rough-hewn, the log is again turned, and the inside cut out with the axe. This operation was formerly done by fire, but the process was slow and tedious. During the chopping the Indian frequently ascertains the thickness of the sides by placing one hand on the outside and the other on the inside. The canoe is now again turned bottom up, and the whole smoothed off with a peculiar-shaped chisel, used something after the manner of a cooper's adze. This is a very tiresome job, and takes a long time. Then the inside is finished, and the canoe now has to be stretched into shape. It is first nearly filled with water, into which hot stones are thrown, and at the same time a fire of bark is built outside. This in a short time renders the wood so supple that the center can be spread open at the top from six inches to a foot. This is kept in place by sticks or stretchers, similar to the method of a boat's thwarts. The ends of these stretchers are fastened by means of withes made from the taper ends of cedar limbs, twisted and used instead of cords. When all is finished, the water is emptied out, and then the stem and head-pieces are put on. These are carved from separate sticks, and are fastened on by means of withes and wooden pegs or tree-nails. After the inside is finished to the satisfaction of the maker, the canoe is again turned, and the charred part, occasioned by the bark fire, is rubbed with stones to make the bottom as smooth as possible, when the whole outside is painted over with a black mixture made of burned rushes and whale oil. The inside is also painted red with a mixture of red ochre and oil. The edges all round are studded with little shells, which are the valve joint of the common snail, and, when brass-headed nails can be obtained, they are used in profusion. This description I give is of the making of a canoe near my house, and I saw the progress every day, from the time the tree was cut down till the canoe was finished. This was a medium sized canoe, and took three months to finish it."

These dugout canoes are still used in northern Washington, although of course, now they are made with modern tools, and sometimes powered with an outboard motor. Excursions can be taken in them down the Quinault River.

THE GREAT PESTILENCE

Late in the summer of 1830, a violent epidemic of "fever and ague" broke out on the lower Columbia, and dealt a fearful blow to the native population of the river between the mouth of the Cowlitz and The Dalles, forever destroying their power; by 1835 the Indians were practically extinct. John K. Townsend, the naturalist, writes: "The Indians of the Columbia were once a numerous and powerful people; the shore of the river, for scores of miles, was lined with their villages; the council fire was frequently lighted, the pipe passed round, and the destinies of the nation deliberated upon. War was declared against neighboring tribes; the deadly tomahawk was lifted, and not buried until it was red with the blood of the savage; the bounding deer was hunted, killed, and his antlers ornamented the wigwam of the red man; the scalps of his enemies hung drying in the smoke of his lodge, and the Indian was happy. Now, alas! where is he? —gone;—gathered to his fathers and to his happy hunting grounds; his place knows him no more. The spot where once stood the thickly populated village, the smoke curling and wreathing above the closely packed lodges, the lively children playing in the front, and their indolent parents lounging on their mats, is now only indicated by a heap of indistinguishable ruins. The depopulation here has been truly fearful." Rev. Samuel Parker says, " I have found the Indian population in the lower country, that is, below the falls of the Columbia, far less than I had expected, or what it was when Lewis and Clark made their tour. Since the year 1829 probably seven-eighths, if not as Doct. McLaughlin believes, nine-tenths, have been swept away by disease, principally by fever and ague. So many and so sudden were the deaths which occurred, that the shores were strewed with the unburied dead. Whole and large villages were depopulated; and some entire tribes have disappeared, the few remaining persons, if there were any, uniting themselves with other tribes."

On Sauvies Island the mortality rate was nearly 100%. In 1835 Dr. McLaughlin had the dead villages burned. Nathaniel Wyeth said: "A mortality has carried off to a man its inhabitants and there is nothing to attest that they ever existed, except their decaying houses, their graves, and their unburied bones, of which there are heaps!" Deer Island, 33 miles below Vancouver, was also decimated, according to Parker: "Deer Island was formerly the residence of many Indians, but they are gone, and nothing is left but the remains of a large village." Sir George Simpson writes: "When I descended the Cowlitz, in 1828, there was a large population along its banks; but since then the intermittent fever, which commenced its ravages in the following year, has left but few to mourn for those that fell. During the whole of our day's course, till we came upon a small camp in the evening, the shores were silent and solitary, the deserted villages forming melancholy monuments of the generation that had passed away." Even to this day every spring freshet of the Columbia uncovers remains of those who lay where they died, and were covered with flood silt.

Local white residents were not exempt. Dr. McLaughlin wrote in 1830: "The Intermitting Fever (for the first time since the trade of this Department was established) has appeared at this place, at present there are fifty-two of our people on the sick list." And David Douglas says, also in 1830: "A dreadful fatal intermittent fever broke out in the lower parts of this river about eleven weeks ago. I am one of the few persons among the Hudson's Bay Company's people who have withstood it." But the malady was not fatal to the white people, although they became very ill there were practically no deaths.

The fearful toll amongst the Indians was due to their method of treatment—a sweat bath followed by a plunge in the river—and their lack of immunity to strange diseases. Actually the sickness was relatively easy to cure. Townsend tells about finding a young girl sick in her lodge, and he cured her in two days with quinine. When his small supply was exhausted he used an infusion of dogwood bark and cured two other children. Quinine was freely used at the Hudson's Bay Post.

The great pestilence is said to have started when the American ship *Owyhee*, of Boston, sailed up the Columbia in 1829 to trade. There was no more reason to suspect this ship than the *Dryad, Isabelle,* or *Vancouver,* all of which were on the river in 1828 and 1830. But these were British ships, and for the purpose of trade it was more convenient to blame the Americans. Some believed it was caused by turning the ground, releasing the disease, for the Hudson's Bay Company started farming that year. The epidemic actually started at Fort Vancouver.

The preponderence of evidence indicates that the disease was malaria. Other suspected causes, cholera, smallpox, plague, measles, and typhus, have been virtually eliminated. There are many references to the sickness in old journals and the symptoms described fit malaria closer than any other disease. Cholera, smallpox, and measles were well known to the whites and would have been recognized, and there were no domestic rats to act as carriers of the plague, although there was no shortage of fleas. There is no mention in discussions of the pestilence of the possibility of a disease related to influenza, which can strike with swift and terrible destruction. The same disease decimated the natives along the Sacramento River, in California, in 1833, and Malaria reached epidemic proportions in the Central Valley again in 1850. Malaria is carried by a certain mosquito, Anaphiles maculipennis, which inhabits only that part of the Columbia from about the Cowlitz River to the vicinity of the Cascades, and a considerable distance up the Willamette. This fact accounts for the relative freedom of the upper river from the epidemic. There are mosquitoes in this area as any camper along the river can attest, but they are not important as malaria carriers. The epidemic seems to have reached down the coast as far as the Rogue River, but apparently not nearly so severe as along the Columbia. The lower Coast Indians were inclined to kill all white men, believing they brought the fatal disease with them. Malaria is no longer known in the Columbia River Valley.

This was the second pestilence suffered by the Indians that was started by the white man. Sometime about 1780 the smallpox raged along the coast and up the Columbia. When the first explorers arrived by land the power of the Indians had already been broken, villages were decimated and some were deserted. No white man ever saw the natives along the river in the full glory of their culture, except possibly some shipwreck survivors who left no record.

One result of the pestilence was that the Columbia and Willamette valleys were settled without the fearful Indian battles so common in other parts of the country. The gold seekers of 1849, in California, were able to explore the hills and valleys without interference from the Indians, quite contrary to the prospectors in the Southwest who risked their lives in search of wealth. The poor specimens of broken tribes described by the pioneers on the Columbia are responsible for the myth that the local Indians were without character and without principles. Lt. Wilkes puts it aptly when he says: "about the Cascades and at The Dalles still linger considerable numbers of this ill fated and fast fading people. There is no longer any spirit left in them; their hearts are broken, their bows unstrung, and from the lords of the soil they have sunk to the degradation of slaves."

A NATIVE FLINT QUARRY

The hundreds of thousands of chipped artifacts found along the Columbia required a considerable source of supply of raw material, particularly since a relatively large portion was waste. Discarded chips lie deep all along the river; in the old campsites they occur in banks where the drifting sands have left them, and their bright colors enlighten the grey gravel on the beaches. There were several sources of supply. Petrified wood is found in many places in the old lava flows where the forests were buried and percolating waters deposited minerals in the wood cells. Colored agate is found in some of the lava and ash beds, and semi-precious stones can be picked up in the gravel, originating perhaps far up in Canada.

Much of the material, however, was mined from seams in the basalt, uncovered with stone slab digging tools and broken from the ledge with stone hammers. One of these ancient quarries is on the cliffs a few miles from the river on Highway 97. The largest yet discovered, and what may be one of the largest in the United States, was found by George Gunkel of Maryhill, Washington, a few miles above The Dalles, on the north bank. Far above the river, for a quarter of a mile along the rocky hillside the Indians have dug holes up to 20 feet deep to uncover a seam of Wascoite, a semi-precious, agatized, multi-colored mineral. The soil was dug and carried out, probably in baskets, and dumped over the bank, and the arrow point material wedged and broken off with stone tools, which still litter the site. Fig. 28 shows one of these ancient mines, one of the many holes along the outcropping. George is standing on the edge and Clifford Dolph, director of the Maryhill Museum, is showing George's son Daniel how the basalt overlays the Wascoite. Along the ridge, out of sight in the foreground, a well worn trail winds down to the river. Hundreds of cubic yards of material have been removed along this seam.

About three miles above this quarry the seam or a similar one again appears, this has been extensively mined for a distance of about 200 yards. A large portion of the chipped work along the river is made of the same type of material that comes from these two mines, and blocks of it have been found in the village sites on Sauvies Island and along the lower Columbia.

Fig. 28

ANCIENT FLINT MINE ON THE COLUMBIA RIVER

PART II
THE CULTURE

PICTURE ROCKS

The most spectacular surviving indication of prehistoric man along the Columbia is the numerous petroglyphs and pictographs on the smooth basalt cliffs through which the river has cut its channel. These dark colored surfaces were ideal for the practice of the art, for the lighter shades beneath made the pictures stand out in bold relief. Many of them are in prominent locations, re-

Fig. 29

PICTURES IN PETROGLYPH CANYON

quiring considerable exertion to reach, as though the artist intended to expose his creation for all to see.

Picture rocks are known throughout the world. Wherever there was a suitable surface and inhabitants with leisure, there are pictures. The reason the Columbia is so rich in them is that the area was so thickly populated, and the smooth basalt cliffs needed for their display extended for miles along the river. Then too the population was sedentary during the fishing season, and there was much leisure time. While the vast majority—and there are thousands of them—are simple designs and pictures of animals, some are works of art with a skill of execution and technique of expression worthy of a high culture.

Fig. 30

LEFT, HUNTING SCENE; RIGHT, PETROGLYPH IN THE LONG NARROWS

Most picture rocks are in the vicinity of good fishing grounds where there was a large summer population, although occasionally one or two are found miles from the river along what were probably trails to the fishing sites. Considering the vast population, the carvings must have been done by a relatively few persons. Petroglyphs, which describes a figure having depth, were made by pecking the surface with a hard river pebble; sometimes these hammers are found where they were used. Generally the carvings are shallow, just beneath the surface, but some are incised a half inch or more deep.

A pictograph is a painting, although sometimes the petroglyphs were also painted after carving. The pigment used was generally one of the iron oxides which occur in several places in Oregon and Washington. They are found in several shades from bright red through yellow to grey. Ochre is a fine clay colored with iron oxide; it varies widely in structure and color. White paint was made of talc, koalin, or white clay. Charcoal and dark earths were used for black. Various shades of blue and green are found in the John Day beds, which are ancient sea deposits. About 90% of the pictographs are red.

Paint was made from the pigments by grinding it fine on a convenient flat stone or in a mortar, then mixing with animal oils and resin from pine trees. Water may have also been used. The mixture was absorbed into the rock and became part of it, lasting for hundreds of years

Fig. 31

MOUNTAIN SHEEP

if reasonably sheltered. On the cliffs at Cape Horn above Camas, Washington, there are some pictographs that appear to be very old but are still quite clear. They are so high on the cliff that the topography must have been different when they were painted, or else ladders were used by the artist. One is on a rock that has fallen onto the river bank and is covered with water part of the year. It is still recognizable.

Application of the paint was by the fingers or a brush made from a bit of hair, or even a pad of fur. Sometimes the artist experimented with his colors and method of application before painting the picture he had in mind, the results thereof are frequently mistaken for a design. The artist had very little respect for his predecessor, many pictographs and petroglyphs are drawn over earlier ones.

Petroglyphs and pictographs are no longer considered to be pictures drawn solely for amusement, but the symbolism has never been worked out to show a connected meaning. Many reports have been published, especially in the newspapers, giving the most absurd interpretations, the product of imagination and romance rather than basic research. The truth is not spectacular and therefore not popular.

Most authorities contend that the intent of some of the designs was to convey a magical or religious meaning. Motifs and styles may be grouped in limited areas, a certain design may have had special significance in that region. The four pointed star and the Spedis owl are typical of a conception limited to the mid-Columbia area. The diamond is a basic design and widespread, but the type shown in Fig. 29 is a special one called a four-pointed star. The owl, also, is a basic symbol, but the treatment of the design on the mid-Columbia is unique and called the Spedis owl. It may have been a clan symbol, or garnished with mystery by the local shaman it would have been looked upon with awe by the local populance, although it may have been carved by some former and forgotten tribe. The first Spedis owl on the river occurs on a large boulder near Skamania on the edge of a large village site (SK 2). In the vicinity of the

TSAGAGLALAL   Fig. 32

Long Narrows there are several of them. The artist had his designs firmly fixed in his mind; all of them are well drawn.

The mountain sheep is by far the most common of the animal motifs and was probably drawn simply from a desire to obtain this elusive animal, valued both for its skin and flesh, much as a modern youth draws pictures of a longed for "hot rod." The salmon on which the natives depended for their very existence was easily taken and pictures of it are comparatively rare. Other basic designs along the Columbia are the circle, circle and dot, ladder, zig zag line, lizard, and sunburst.

The most spectacular of all the carvings is called Tsagaglalal, "She Who Watches." This combination petroglyph and pictograph, a petroglyph that has been painted with red ochre, is on a cliff overlooking the village site at the Long Narrows, and is one of best examples of aboriginal art in the United States. It is executed in the characteristic Columbia River style, with circled eyes and mouth elements found on many bone and rock carvings. This is the legend of Tsagaglalal:

> A woman had a house where the village of Nixluidix was later built. She was chief of all who lived in this region. That was a long time before Coyote came up the river and changed things and people were not yet real people. After a time Coyote in his travels came to this place and asked the inhabitants if they were living well or ill. They sent him to their chief who lived up on the rocks, where she could look down on the village and know what was going on. Coyote climbed up to the house on the rocks and asked "What kind of living do you give these people? Do you treat them well or are you one of those evil women?" "I am teaching them to live well and build good houses," she said. "Soon the world will change," said Coyote, "and women will no longer be chiefs." Then he changed her into a rock with the command,

"You shall stay here and watch over the people who live here." All the people know that Tsagaglalae sees all things, for whenever they are looking at her those large eyes are watching them.

Just above the start of the Long Narrows a series of low cliffs overlooking the river was called Petroglyph Canyon because of the many carvings there. All are now under water except six that were removed by the National Park Service, a few saved by The Dalles Museum Commission, and a couple that were lifted by someone for souvenirs for their rock garden; a sad fate for these historical monuments, out of their rugged settings they are but poor representations of a romantic past.

About one mile above Upper Memaloose Island there was a peninsula called Crawford's Point that had a number of exceptionally fine specimens, and Brown's Island was covered with them. Others are at Cliffs, the John Day bar, opposite Blalock, and at Roosevelt. On the upper

Fig. 33

SMALL BONE CARVING IN IMITATION OF TSAGAGLALAL. Natural size.

river there is a group at Page on the Snake, and one near
Vantage, soon to be drowned in the backwaters of a dam.
There were a number of Rock Island Rapids near We-
natchee, some of these were saved before Rock Island
Dam was built. These are the places where they were
concentrated, many are scattered along the river above
Vancouver, where the first ones appear.

Fig. 34

PETROGLYPHS ON THE LONG NARROWS

None of the early writers mention petroglyphs except
Wilkes, who tells of "hierloglyphic rocks" several miles
above the John Day River. These could have been none
other than the group opposite Blalock.

Petroglyphs and pictographs photograph beautifully in
color, providing you can get there before someone has
chalked them in. The busy snap shot artist with a bit of
chalk is the bane of the serious photographer, he leaves

not the original picture but his interpretation of it, and has for his reward only a record of his dexterity with the crayon. Ordinary chalk will wash off in a season, but some use wax crayon, which spoils the picture for a long time. In color, they should be photographed in direct sunlight. In black and white most of them show up better with side lighting, when the carving is in relief.

The age of petroglyphs is difficult to estimate. Some are obviously recent, pictures of men on horseback cannot be over a couple of hundred years old. Others are nearly eroded away, indicating respectable antiquity. Weathering and erosion are not conclusive evidence of age because of the inequalities of the rock and difference of exposure. However, when weathered and fresh petroglyphs are in the same area such as Petroglyph Canyon, there must be considerable difference in age, still with no indication of the extent of the difference. The weathered ones are frequently merely random lines pecked in the rock,

Fig. 35

ELK PICTOGRAPH

perhaps they were inscribed prior to the cultural upheaval that produced the finest specimens, along with the stone and bone creations found in the camp sites. A good example may be found on the top of the cliff at Big Eddy, directly above the famous Elk pictograph (Fig. 35). Others are on Telephone Island near Patterson. The only dependable method of dating is by association with known design elements such as the exposed skeleton motif. Petroglyphs with this design cannot be over about 1,200 years old, but also may be much younger. Authorities believe the art became extinct about the time of the white invasion. Modern Indians disclaim all knowledge of the origin or meaning of the pictures and symbols, and sometimes regard them with superstitious awe as marks of the "old people."

Fig. 29 shows a few of the hundreds of pictures from Petroglyph Canyon. In the upper left is a typical Spedis owl, a lizard design, and the four-pointed star. The figure in the upper right is one of the best in the area, it also has an appearance of greater age than the others. Note the elaborate head dress. In the lower left is another lizard or "water devil" design, mountain goats, and a wavy line that may represent a snake. In the lower right are two elaborate zoomorphic figures. Just above the upper figure is a pair of circled eyes, a common design in The Dalles area. Also shown are the random markings and crude designs that appear on many rocks, the finer pictures frequently overlay these simple markings.

The top picture of Fig. 34 shows two Spedis owls, an elk, and a group of mountain sheep, also a pair of well executed elk or deer tracks. In the lower left is one of the most outstanding and deepest incised figures in Petroglyph Canyon. Certainly the artist who created this design had a definite concept in mind. It was on the top of a steep cliff overlooking the water—and the only way to get a picture of it was to hold the camera out over the edge of the cliff and shoot backwards. This specimen was removed by some unknown person for a souvenir. The

design in the lower right picture was on the rocks opposite the upper end of the Long Narrows, on the Oregon
shore.
In Fig. 30, top, is shown a hunting scene. The hunter
has a bow and arrow and his quarry is four mountain
sheep (or elk) ; he is assisted by three dogs. Scenes depict-
ing actual events are not plentiful on the river. In the
group opposite Blalock there are two similar hunting
scenes, and at the mouth of the John Day River there was
a hunter slaying a mountain sheep with a bow and arrow,
and a fisherman with a dip net containing a salmon. The
carved rock in Fig. 30, bottom, was on a small rock
island in the center of the Long Narrows. It is not in its
original position, having fallen on its side. The rock is
covered with water during flood stages, and even in low
water the violent currents make access difficult. Few people have seen this creation, and it is now under 60 feet
of water.

James Hansen, sculptor of Vancouver, Washington,
originated a method of making wax impressions of
petroglyphs from which, by means of a flexible die and
a special casting compound, duplicate copies can be made
that are in appearance exactly like the originals. Spon-
sored by the Oregon Museum of Science and Industry,
Mr. Hansen made casts of a number of the better petroglyphs before they were inundated by the waters behind
The Dalles Dam. Copies are available from the Museum.

COLUMBIA RIVER ART

Art, according to Webster's Dictionary, is the disposition or modification of things by means of human skill,
and consists of two parts, mechanical by which the hands
and body are more concerned than the mind, and fine
arts such as give scope to genius. The latter has an aesthetic
quality, it is an expression of emotion and deep feeling
and often is created for the sake of art itself. This latter
form is scarce in Indian culture, instead it takes the form

of embellishment of utilitarian objects far beyond that required by good workmanship. The art we are concerned with here is prehistoric. Much of the familiar Indian art, such as totem poles and jewelry, is post-contact, and encouraged and fostered by the white man.

Fig. 36

HUMAN HEAD CARVINGS

Many of the Columbia River sculptures serve no utilitarian purpose and can be classed as aesthetic. Bone figurines are found that are carved with mechanical precision, frequently with interlocked designs that display a mastery of technique and expression of talent seldom encountered in primitive art. Large stones are given animal or fish forms, and a number of carved heads, sometimes highly conventionalized, have been found representing mountain sheep, human, and purely stylized forms. These objects served no useful purpose.

One does not have to be an art student to appreciate art, or to recognize its simplest forms, a category in which much primitive art falls. It can be enjoyed without knowing its features, for these can be felt without being consciously classified into their respective elements. The most primitive people were creative and developed forms that although crude and simple, gave them aesthetic pleasure. There are, however, certain fundamental characteristics of true art, and a knowledge of them may help one to appreciate the wonderful specimens of primitive art found on the Columbia.

First, the form should appeal to the senses, in this case to the sight and touch. The primitive artist, no matter how strong the urge to express himself aesthetically, or how original or talented his feeling for form, was helpless without the mechanical skill to transfer his thoughts into a fixed development. Without the patience and technical ability there could be no expression. The symbolic bowl in the lower left of Fig. 71, is a good example of the combination of feeling for form and the skill to express it.

This bowl is carved from granite, a material requiring considerable effort to shape. With a picture of the finished product constantly in his mind, this primitive artist selected a boulder from the thousands lying on the river bank and with a quartzite pebble patiently pecked away a few grain at a time. With skill and taste he spaced the projecting elements, the head rises above and is spaced midway between the two feet, balanced on the opposite side with a round projecting tail. The eyes protrude; it would have been much easier to round off the head and then peck in depressions for them. The bowl portion is perfectly circular, the pattern evenly spaced. One cannot but marvel at not only the skill but the prodigious patience of the creator of this masterpiece. There have been many objects found on the river that were produced by artists whose aesthetic feeling must have been equal to or greater than this one but who lacked the skill to express it. Technical skill, then, is a necessary attribute to the achievement of art expression.

The technical skill of formal art is used to attain symmetry and rhythm. Symmetry may be acquired in many ways, there may be equal right and left halves, or a division about a vertical line, the most usual method. There may be a symmetrical pattern in a circle like the decoration on a bowl. The stone atlatl weights, Fig. 66, have symmetry about the central groove, the form is pleasing both to the sight and touch. The most remarkable examples of symmetry in Columbia River art are the delicate bone carvings like the one in the center of the bottom row of Fig. 41, and those in Fig. 42. Technical skill reached perfection in these pieces. There is symmetry in arrow points and knives. The work expended on some of these was solely to produce a pleasing form; the chipping

Fig. 37

STONE MORTARS

produced a pattern and the stone was chosen for its beauty, and frequently shaped to utilize some flaw or configuration in the structure to emphasize the design. I have never seen an arrow point in an art museum, which is a pity, for some of them are masterpieces of the control of technique and expression of form.

Rhythm may be attained by a repetition of pattern, a method most frequently applied to basketry. The best chipped pieces show a repetition of evenly spaced, equal flaking. Stone bowls frequently utilize this method, the one in the upper left of Fig. 71 has an evenly spaced, flowing pattern, not elaborate but skillfully applied to emphasize the outlines of the bowl. This is another frequently utilized technique, emphasizing form by a pattern. Representative art is a familiar object in symbolic form. A realistic picture, such as the elk in Fig. 35, is not necessarily representative art, but the bird effigy mortars in Fig. 39 are. The details of the subjects are lacking or of minor importance, the main features are forcibly expressed. Formal art is concerned with form alone, like a beautifully shaped adze blade, or a polished maul, for instance. Representative art is a concept combined with form, and is the ultimate in primitive art. The object has an aesthetic value and a perfection of form in representative art. The bird and animal effigy mortars were executed not as a mere picture but because the subject had some emotional appeal. The bowl in Fig. 71, lower right, is a good example. All detail is suppressed, realism is entirely non-existent, the interest is centered on form only.

Columbia River art has a definite style, the result, perhaps, of long tradition, which automatically indicates considerable antiquity. Art, as well as all other cultural traits, is the product of history. There must have been primitive Michelangelo's, as well as Isaac Newton's, who rose above the multitude in comparative scale. It may be that Tsagaglalal was created by such a man and his work widely imitated on bone and stone carvings, for example Fig 33, thus creating a new phase of an old tradition. The characteristics of Columbia River art are massive form and directness of expression. Like the Northwest Coast and Mayan art, it can be recognized and segregated. Douglas and D'Harnoncourt, authors of *Indian Art of the United States*, say that Indian art partakes of the region and its people. The agricultural inhabitants of the Southwest created abstract designs on their pottery; the hunters of the Northwest Coast shaped monumental zoomorphic representations. The natives of the Columbia developed a bold and impressive style.

The most characteristic feature of this style is the representation of the rib structure on practically all human, animal, and fish forms. Sometimes this feature is subdued

Fig. 38

THE FLUTE PLAYER

and sometimes it is so emphasized that it practically excludes all other features. Another is the prominent, pro-

Fig. 39

SMALL STONE MORTARS

truding, bulging eyes. There are several minor characteristics, among them the "grinning face," elaborate ear ornaments, and prominent orbital ridges, but these are not
constant.

Although the Mid-Columbia area had been occupied for
thousands of years, it was not until possibly 1,500 years
ago that the cultural era was established that resulted in
the most spectacular creations of The Dalles region. The
era reached its climax about 500 years ago; it was then
that the blending of cultural traits resulted in the most
elaborate art forms. The Long Narrows was already a
great trade mart, a meeting place of distant tribes with
subsequent exchange of traditions, and it is there that
most of the art work is found. The characteristic Columbia River style was established during this time.

The expression took several forms; there are thousands
of petroglyphs and pictographs, many small bone carvings, and elaborate stone work. Stone was only one of the
materials used by the Indians for their carvings; while it
is the one not subject to deterioration by the elements
and so is the only one—except occasional bone—now
found, actually wood was used far more extensively. Fig.
24 is one example of the expression in wood that has
been preserved; elaborate carved wooden bowls, spoons,
and other implements were common in prehistoric times.
Early writers were united in their praise of native canoes,
highly carved and decorated, while many mention carved
and painted wood boards and figures in and about their
houses and burial vaults. Baskets and woven hats were
frequently decorated. The creative era apparently lasted
until the cultural upheaval occasioned by the white invasion, culminated by the small pox epidemic of about
1780 and the great plague of 1829-1830.

The common stylistic element of Columbia River art,
the exposed rib motif, is seen in the bone carving in the
upper left of Fig. 41, as well as the elaborate ear ornamentation frequently encountered. The large crescent mouth
or "grinning face" is seen on Tsagaglalal, Fig. 32, and

SMALL STONE CARVINGS   Fig. 40

the small bone carving, Fig. 33. The eyes are prominent and protruding, and surrounded with a bold orbital ridge. Traces of red paint show that some of the sculptures were deeply colored.

The objects of aesthetic art are rare except in the Sauvies Island area and in the vicinity of The Dalles. In other places the expression takes the form of decoration of utilitarian objects, which of course appear with the aesthetic forms. Hand mauls seem to have been the favorite tool for decorating; the handle end is often carved in the form of a bird or animal head, or has a simple knob or ringed design. The long "Salmon packer" pestles were also decorated, and slate effigies, Fig. 91, are found throughout the area above Hood River.

The massive style of Columbia River art is well illustrated by the two human head forms shown in Fig. 36. The one on the left is part of a mortar made of lava and stands twelve inches high. For simplicity and impressive dignity this work stands alone in primitive art. The fragmentary face on the right is also part of a mortar carved of lava. The lips are polished and stained with red ochre. Certainly this creation should be classed with the finest examples of Columbia River art. Both were found by Lloyd and Harry McLeod on the Oregon shore of the Columbia near The Dalles.

In Fig. 39 are shown some examples of decorated small mortars, a favorite medium for art expression. The one on the upper left was found in Wakemap Mound by Harold Lee, it is a stylized eagle or other bird; the handle represents the beak, and the projection on the opposite side, the tail; eyes are shown on the body near the handle. The vertical lines are stylized ribs. The artisan who created this piece never saw a handled cup. The zoomorphic mortar on the upper right was found by Mr. and Mrs. Fred Harrison in the yard of their home at the mouth of the John Day River. Mortars with legs are rare on the River, and this is one of the finest ever found. It is at this time on display at the Maryhill Museum of Fine Arts.

Fig. 41

SMALL BONE CARVINGS

The two on the bottom were found by the McLeods near The Dalles. The stylized eagle is four inches high, it has a beak and also a mouth; the circled, protruding eyes are characteristic of the Columbia River style. The one on the right is seven and a half inches long and probably represents a beaver, as the tail is broad and incised with lines. It is similar in style to the one shown in Fig. 71, which came from the same area.

The work shown in Fig. 37 is 17 inches high, of vesicular lava, and is from the McLeod collection. It is carved in an adaptation of the Columbia River style; the ribs and backbone are evident but the eye treatment is unique. The elaborate ear or hair ornamentation is shown, as well as a head dress. A very intelligent Indian woman said this piece represents Coyote playing a flute. There have been two other works found with a similar motif, one of which is in the Portland Art Museum.

In Figs. 40, 41 and 42, are examples of small stone and bone carvings, one of the most elaborate forms. The face on the upper left of Fig. 40 is made of green serpentine, and is two and three-quarters inches wide. It was found by Stuart Thompson in the Congdon site, perhaps the best carved amulet ever found along the Columbia, and truly an artistic creation. The steatite figurine on the right is four inches high, and was found at the mouth of the John Day by the Harrisons. It is not carved in the Columbia River style but appears to be a local production. The holes for suspension piercing the ear ornamentation are worn nearly through and new ones have been drilled near the chin, showing that it had been worn for a long time. The animal head on the lower right was found by Charles Hall at the mouth of the Deschutes River, and he also found the one on the lower left, which is less than an inch long. The stylized mountain sheep head comes from the McLeod collection.

Typical bone carvings are shown in Fig. 41. The one on the upper left was found in Wakemap Mound by Mr.

and Mrs. Harold Wernex, it was probably a hair ornament but may have been a head scratcher. This specimen
is five and a quarter inches long. The carved elkhorn
animal in the top center was found by Charles Selby on
the Oregon shore, about five miles below The Dalles in

Fig. 42

BONE FIGURINES

a highway excavation. The tang is notched as though
made to be lashed to a staff. The figure on the upper
right is carved on the end of a needle or blanket pin that
is nine and a half inches long; the design is a human head
surmounted by a stylized animal. It was found deep in
Wakemap Mound by Carrel Morton. The detail is excellent. Lower left, from the Hall collection, and lower
right, found by Frank Wilke, are small bone pendants
and came from Wakemap Mound. In the center, from
the Harrison collection, is one of the famed bone carvings

found in cremations in The Dalles area. Unfortunately, these delicate specimens are always badly shattered and burned, some of the better preserved specimens are shown in Fig. 42, from the Leachman-St. Clair collection.

PERSONAL ADORNMENT

When a proud people have a favorable economy they always spend considerable effort on personal adornment, and in few places was "making a living" as easy as on the Columbia, with its unlimited supply of salmon. The main articles of adornment—the feathers, fur, porcupine quills, paint and tatooing, shell, bone, and wood—have disappeared long ago, but a great variety of stone objects is found that effectively portray native skill and patience in forming ornaments to be worn on the person or clothing.

Of these objects that yet survive by far the most plentiful are stone beads. They occur in a great variety of shapes and sizes, from a tenth of an inch in length and

Fig. 43

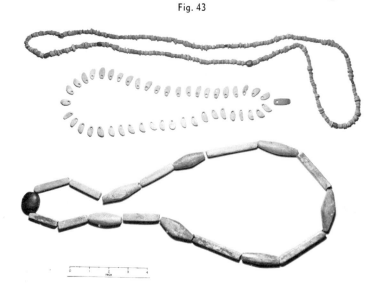

INDIAN MADE BEADS

diameter, to four inches long and a quarter of an inch square. They are found throughout the length of the river but occur in quantity only in the vicinity of the Long Narrows, where they are found in astonishing numbers. Just downstream from The Dalles Bridge, on the Oregon side, was a site called the Bead Patch because of the quantities found there. Covering several acres, it was in the shape of a low mound with a midden up to six feet deep. Excavation was started in 1927 and continued until recently when the area was turned into a gun club. Most of the beads were found in the top two feet, intermixed with large rocks. It is very probable that this was a burying ground superimposed on a still older camp ground, and so old that no evidence of graves was left; the screeners thought that they were working a concentrate left by the winds blowing away the sand. The late Robert Miller, who spent many days working there, estimated that the stone beads found in this ancient site would make a string over a thousand feet long.

Another site prolific in beads was Indian Well, described elsewhere in this book. The Congdon site produced a quantity of the larger beads but practically no small ones. The Big Leap had a few hundred medium sized beads, and the Maybe site a couple of hundred large ones. Each site was different as far as beads were concerned. Indian Well produced small ones only, the Bead Patch both large and small, Congdon medium sized, and Maybe all large. Atlatl Valley had none at all, and no other known site on the river produces more than a few. Wakemap Mound had practically none.

Columbia River stone beads are practically all made from one of the soapstones, usually steatite, but sometimes green serpentine and hard coal were used. Steatite and serpentine are found in the vicinity of Blewett Pass and Kettle Falls in Washington, and Grants Pass and John Day in Oregon. Those made from the hard materials such as agate are unknown, or at least not reported, although there is a copper bead in the Sams collection that appears to be native. The hole is drilled from each side and is cup shaped, a form assumed when a drill of wood using sand as an abrasive is used. Beads of rock crystal, cornelian, and other extremely hard materials have been found in other parts of North America.

To make beads the worker sawed off a slab of the selected stone corresponding to the desired length or width of the bead, then cut it into sections and drilled them. After drilling, the bead was dressed down with abrasive stones to the desired shape. Small beads were strung on a sliver or thong and dressed down all at once. Fig. 86

Fig. 44

STONE AGE ORNAMENTS

shows an abrasive stone used for the final polishing of large beads, which were found with it and fit the indentation in the slab.

The natives used a number of drilling techniques. The Columbia River beads have never been studied to determine the method used here. One method was to use a stone drill chipped from one of the flints. It was lashed to a stick and twirled between the palms, the shaft alter-

Fig. 45

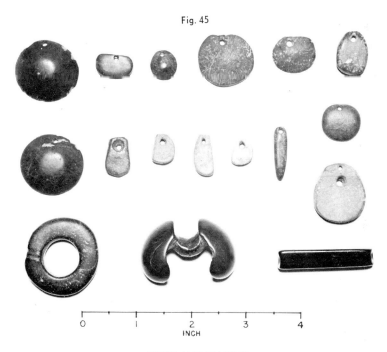

BEADS AND BANGLES

nating in direction of rotation. The bow drill and the pump drill are prehistoric implements and may have been used on the river. The bow drill was made by wrapping the bow string once around the drill shaft and drawing the bow back and forth, causing the shaft to turn rapidly in alternating directions. A block of wood hollowed out to fit the upper end of the shaft was used to hold it in position and impart pressure. The drill bit was a chipped stone, or wood with sand as an abrasive. This type of drill required some device or an assistant to hold the object being drilled, unless the block was made to be held in the teeth as is done by the Eskimo.

The pump drill is a shaft with a disc near its lower end to act as a flywheel. A string is attached by its center to the upper end of the shaft, the ends are tied to a cross bar a foot or so long. The shaft is turned by hand until the string is wrapped around it, then downward pressure on the cross bar causes the string to unwind rapidly and spin the shaft; the momentum of the disc rewinds the string for another down stroke, causing the shaft to turn in the opposite direction.

Abrasive drilling was done by using a hollow reed, twirling it in the presence of sand. The reed used was soft enough for the sand to become imbedded in it; if too hard, it would wear rapidly. In drilling small holes in hard material the hole made when using a stick as an abrasive drill would become conical as the stick wore down, but in soft material the hole might be nearly cyndrical. It is known that this method was used on the Columbia, pipes and some of the large beads show evidence of the reed abrasive drill.

The small beads are one tenth to one quarter inch in diameter and from one twentieth to one sixteenth inch thick, circular, and flat, as shown in the lower right of Fig. 44. They average 14 to the inch when strung. Round and barrel shaped beads occur in all sizes up to about one-half inch in diameter, occasionally one is found an inch or more in diameter. The large beads are nearly always square, drilled from each end, and vary from one to four inches long. Some are prism shaped, square in cross section, with the center about twice as large in diameter as the ends. The small flat beads have been found stuck together side by side, indicating that they were worn on a string as a necklace. Large beads found in graves show that they were most frequently worn singly, sometimes in twos or threes. The hole in many is worn on one side of the two ends as it would be if worn singly. They are occasionally found, however, in quantities indicating a full or partial string. One type of bead is flat, kidney shaped, and has two holes. Those found in situ show that they were strung side by side on two strings. Another type is similar in shape but has only one hole at one end; they were also strung side by side. Ornamented beads are rare, occasionally one is found with incised lines. In Fig. 44 are shown four from the Maybe site that are decorated with a flowing design. These are from the McLeod collection.

Fig. 46

CARVED STONE RINGS

Bangles or pendants are made of the same material as beads and are found with them. The most common type is about three quarters of an inch in diameter, flat on one side and rounded on the other, slightly oval shaped, and with a very small hole. Some of them have one or more holes that have worn through and new ones drilled, showing that they were worn for a long time and not just on special occasions. Besides the oval shaped ones there are many other shapes, depending entirely on the originality of the maker. Some of them show real artistic merit. A few are shown in the chapter on art (Fig. 40). Another type of bangle is a plain stone ring made of steatite, beautifully formed and highly polished. They occur in

sizes from four and a half inches in diameter (Fig. 14),
down to what might be considered a large bead. Marks
and indentations on some show that they were worn suspended on a thong, on others there are no marks whatever
to show how they were worn.

Fig. 47

CHIPPED ORNAMENTS

Rings are quite rare. The most of those found came
from the Congdon and Indian Well sites, but a few have
been found elsewhere, practically all of them in The
Dalles area. Fig. 46 shows a pair of carved rings found
together in the Indian Well site. One of them has an
incised line around the outside; it may have been decorative or possibly to hold a suspension cord.

Fig. 47 shows some chipped ornaments that were found
in a position indicating that they were suspended from a
cord and used as a necklace. Their shape indicates that
they were not made for arrow points, the base is rounded
and would have been difficult to haft, while it would have
been ideal for suspending on a cord. The use of chipped
stone for personal adornment was rare, if used at all.

In Fig. 44, upper left, are shown some unusual bangles made of pure, soft graphite, a mineral found not closer than Dillon, Montana. The material is as soft as an artists crayon and must have left a definite mark when worn. Although graphite can be easily worked, none of this material was ever carved or shaped; known artifacts are simply natural pieces that have been drilled. These were found in all sites on the Long Narrows, but not in quantity, a half dozen or so in each. The bead in the lower left of Fig. 44 is an unusual type; two of these were found in the Congdon site. There is a hole drilled through each end with a slot between for the string. They could have been worn singly only.

At the bottom of Fig. 44 are shown some stone age ornaments of bone and shell. They are, left to right, canine tooth, bear claw, eagle talon, elk tooth, shell disc beads, glycymneris shell, abalone shell, and olivella shell.

COLUMBIA RIVER PIPES

(Bowen collection)

The origin of the custom of smoking is lost in antiquity. While the use of the tobacco plant for smoking originated in the Americas, there is evidence that smoking in some form of certain herbs and extracts was performed prior to the Christian era in Asia and Africa, but not in Europe. The word tobacco comes from an Arawak word "tobago", which was the name of an instrument used in snuffing a powder made of the tobacco plant, a custom not indulged in by the Indians north of Mexico. Both smoking and snuffing were described by the Span-

Fig. 48

TOP, CLOUD BLOWERS; BOTTOM, TUBE PIPES

iards during the conquest of the Aztecs, and there are
carved Aztec panels showing the use of the pipe. It is
believed that the custom of smoking solely as a habit and
pastime was originated by the Europeans, and that smoking was more of a ceremonial fashion with the Indians

prior to the white invasion, although they did also smoke for the pleasure of it.

Smoking received its greatest impetus in Europe during the plague, after tobacco was introduced from the Americas, because of the wonderful properties ascribed to it. It was said to cure and prevent disease, and to relieve the pangs of hunger and fatigue, and it was prescribed as an antidote for the plague. It eventually became a habit that, says Washington Irving, "the ingenious caprice of man has converted into a luxury in defiance of the opposition of the senses".

Pipes are found throughout the United States in a variety of shapes and sizes, but the most usual type is the plain tube. Since smoking was ceremonial, pipes were one of the favorite articles for extensive decoration and embellishment, and a common grave offering. Many

Fig. 49

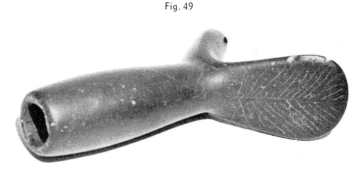

UNUSUAL TYPE OF PIPE FROM THE LONG NARROWS

materials were used in their construction, various kinds of stone, clay, wood, and bone; the stone of course is the only material that has survived the elements in any quantity. Even metal was sometimes used. Pipes have been found made of copper, and trade pipes were made of pewter.

Columbia River pipes are found in many different sizes, from one-half inch to ten inches long, and in several styles which fall into two main groups: the tube and the elbow, with the tube by far the most common. The elbow is shaped like the modern tobacco pipe, and is comparatively rare along the river. One type of elbow pipe is found only in the area near the mouth of the Umatilla River. The bowl is gouged out barrel-shaped and joins the stem at about a 45 degree angle, see Fig. 51, No. 7. There is a fish tail handle under the bowl, with a hole for suspension. Another elbow pipe of unusual construction is shown in Fig. 49; it was found by Frank Sauke in the Maybe site. It is made of hard brown slate, beautifully shaped and polished. The bowl is bored and gouged, the stem bored. The bowl is three and three quarters inches long, the stem one and a half, and the handle or decoration two and a quarter inches long. A small fragment of a similar one, except without the handle, was found in the same place. It appeared never to have been smoked.

One type of tube pipe, Fig. 48, is called a "Cloud blower", it is heavy and thick and made of sandstone or other fine grained rock, and looks similar to those found throughout the United States. It comes from the older sites along the river and is supposed to predate the elbow and tube, but this has not been proven. They were found in the Congdon, Maybe, Indian Well, and Big Leap sites at the Long Narrows and Celilo. They are generally short, practically just bowl. They were not smoked, the bowl was applied to the lips and smoke blown through the stem into the room as a sort of incense to help the shaman in his rites. "Cloud blowers" are seldom decorated but often well made and polished.

The typical Columbia River tube pipe is made of steatite, or chlorite chist, occasionally highly carved and decorated, and beautifully formed and polished; some are so thin as to be translucent when lit. One type has a large flaring base, it is called a wineglass pipe. Most of the tube pipes have a flaring mouthpiece of some kind with a hole drilled through it for the insertion of a suspension cord. Some tube pipes are made to be used with a separate wood or bone stem, and occasionally one is found with a separate stem made of stone. A pebble was dropped into the bottom of the bowl of tube pipes before filling with tobacco to prevent particles from being drawn into the mouth of the smoker. Pipes have been found with the pebble still in place.

Fig. 50

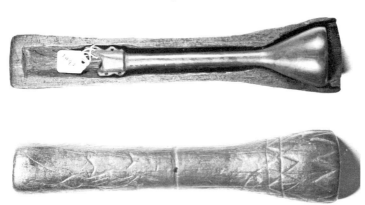

THE MOSES COULEE PIPE

Pipe fragments that were broken during manufacture show that the hole was bored through, using a cane with sand as an abrasive, after the pipe was roughly blocked out. The bowl was then gouged out with a sharp flint, and the pipe shaped. The tools used for bringing the pipe to form were stone scrapers and knives, and abrasives. For the final operations small abrasive stones were used. They have been found round, flat, and wedge shaped. Some sort of very fine abrasive was used for the final polishing, and years of use further polished the already lustrous surface. Pipes have been found with incised decorations worn nearly completely away, indicating long use.

The most spectacular pipe ever found on the Columbia is known as the Moses Coulee pipe. Moses Coulee is an

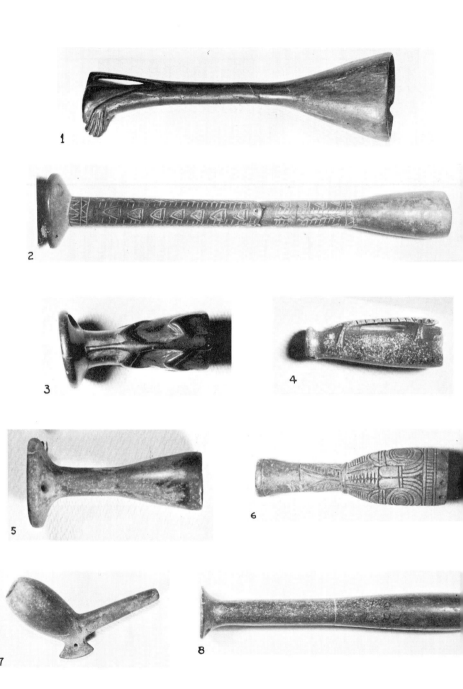

Fig. 51   COLUMBIA RIVER PIPES

ancient bed of the Columbia, cut during the ice age, near Wenatchee, Washington, and named after a prominent Indian chief. Eight miles up the coulee is a large cave that a local rancher cleaned out with a team and scraper so it could be used for storage. Four and one-half feet below the original surface he found in a niche in the wall a bundle of sage brush bark in which was enclosed this remarkable pipe in a carved wooden box, the only instance known that a pipe was cased in wood. The depth at which it was found indicates considerable age, at least several hundred years. It is nearly eight inches long with a large bell shaped bowl, artistically formed and highly polished. The case is eleven inches long, hollowed out to fit the pipe, and carved with v-shaped grooves on the belled end and human-like figures on the body. It is stained dark with use and age but is in perfect condition, as the cave in which it was found was completely dry. It is now owned by Alan G. May of Monitor, Washington, and is on display at the North Central Washington Museum at Wenatchee.

Pipes are very scarce on the lower Columbia, west of the Cascades. It is probable that the wooden pipe was used. Fragments of stone pipes and an occasional whole one are found in the Sauvies Island area, but considering the enormous quantity of other artifacts found there, they are extremely rare. In the vicinity of the Long Narrows they occur more frequently, and the quantity increases toward the upper river.

Early writers describe wooden pipes used by the Chinooks; none of course has survived. Spier and Sapir say that only the shamans and chiefs smoked, the shaman to strengthen his spirit before beginning a cure, and the chiefs during council meetings, passing the pipe around the circle. Archaeological findings seem to indicate that smoking was more common than their informants implied.

In Fig. 48 are shown some "cloud blowers" from the McLeod collection, found in the Big Leap site. The tube pipes shown are from the Maybe site, the dark colored one is 4.9 inches long and has a hole 0.35 inches in diameter, bored straight through, then gouged out to 0.7 inches at the bowl end. The light colored one is 4.6 inches long, with a 0.2 inch hole bored from the bowl end to within 0.9 inches of the stem end, then a 0.3 inch hole bored to meet it at a slight angle. Marks of the abrasive can still be plainly seen in the bore. The bowl is cup shaped, 1.1 inches deep. The short pipe is made for use with a separate wooden or bone stem and still has red paint on it. The place in which it was found indicates an age of several hundred years, at least.

Some of the better examples of Columbia River pipes are shown in Fig. 51. No. 1 is from the Cowles collection. It is from the Vantage area and is a little over seven inches long. The mouthpiece is in the form of the feet and tail of a bird. No. 2 came from the vicinity of the Long Narrows many years ago, and is now owned by Charles Hall. It is nine inches long. It had been broken and repaired by inserting a hollow wooden plug and lacing the two pieces together over it. No. 3, found by Guy Travis near Blalock Island, and No. 4, from the Arch M. Sams collection, and found near North Bonneville, are lizard effigy pipes. The one owned by Mr. Travis has an identical lizard on the opposite side, a beautiful piece of work. No. 7, from the Cowles collection, is one of the elbow pipes from the Umatilla area, previously described. No. 6, from the Charles Hall collection, is a good example of the highly decorated pipes that are occasionally found. The carving is similar to the famous miniature bone carvings found in The Dalles area, where this pipe was unearthed. Note the symmetry and perfection of the design. No. 5 is a typical wineglass pipe, from the Vernon Borden collection. No. 8 is the most usual form and is called the Columbia River tube pipe. This one is from the Morton collection.

The Indians used many plants for smoking. The native tobacco (Nicotiana quadrivalvis) was the only domestic plant cultivated by the western Indians. They planted it in beds of ashes where a log or stump had been burned. Willow bark, kinnikinnick, and even wood was mixed with the tobacco. The method of smoking was to draw in huge lungfulls, until the smoker became dizzy or even insensible. Lewis and Clark state in their *Journals*: "The Chinnooks and others inhabiting the coast and country in this neighborhood, are excessively fond of smoking tobacco. in the act of smoking they appear to swallow it as they draw it from the pipe, and for many draughts together you will not perceive the smoke which they take from the pipe; in the same manner also they inhale it in their lungs untill they become surcharged with this vapour when they puff it out to a great distance through their nostrils and mouth; I have no doubt the smoke of the tobacco in this manner becomes much more intoxicating and that they do possess themselves of all it's virtues in their fullest extent; they frequently give us sounding proofs of it's creating a dismorallity of order in the abdomen." But near the mouth of the Yakima River they say "dureing these preparations I smoked with those about me who chose to smoke which was but fiew, this being a custom those people are but little accustomed to and only smok thru form." It seems that smoking customs varied between the tribes.

CLUBS

Club type weapons are found on the Columbia in several different types but are relatively scarce. The most spectacular is a bladed style called by professionals and amateurs a "slave killer". The name is probably more romantic than factual, as there is no direct evidence that such was their primary function. Occasionally a slave was sacrificed upon the death of his master or for some ceremonial occasion, and it would have been natural to use a "dress" weapon such as these clubs for the purpose. Slaves were a valuable piece of property, at least as long as they were useful, and not to be disposed of with impun-

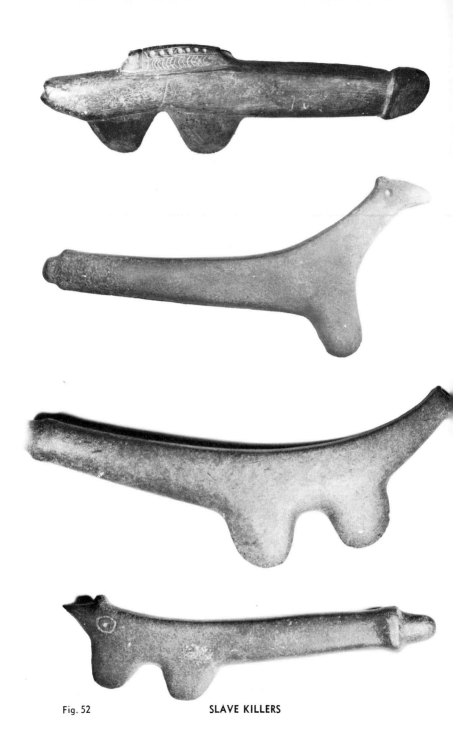

Fig. 52   SLAVE KILLERS

ity by a people lacking the intense social rivalry of the North
Coast tribes, where it was common for an owner to sacri-
fice his slaves merely to show his contempt for wealth and
to shame his rivals. With the love of ceremony characteristic of those people a ceremonial club of some sort would
have been used for the fatal stroke. George Marshall reports that he saw a slave killer at Wrangell, Alaska, but
none are illustrated in books on Northwest Coast art, although Dr. Invararity in *Art of the Northwest Coast
Indians* shows a daggerlike weapon which he calls a slave
killer.

Very few slave killers have been found along the Columbia. Five were washed out from one village site on
Sauvies Island, and a fragment was found in another. I
know of only four complete ones and fragments of three
or four others found at The Dalles, but there were probably more found years ago. Two came from the mouth of
the John Day River and one near McNary Dam, and
three came from near Antelope. Those found in the past
century and the early part of this one have become scattered. There are several in museums throughout the
country. But the total number is not large, probably not
over a couple of dozen have been found along the river.

These clubs may have one, two, or three blades, although the two bladed style is the most common. They
are generally made of some dark colored sedimentary
rock, and all are nicely formed and polished. A few are
decorated with small notches cut into the neck or body.
All have a zoomorphic motif, generally monolithic, but
the splendid one found at the mouth of the John Day,
Fig. 52, top, has a superimposed figure, carved in the characteristic Columbia River style with the exposed skeleton.
This one has features not found in other slave killers that
come from the Columbia region. There is a hole in the
handle for a suspension thong, the others have a rounded
knob, frequently unpolished as though intended to be
wrapped or bound. It does not have the "blood groove",
an incised groove down the full length of the back that is

on all others. The only feature in common with the usual
type is the double blade. There is no doubt that this one
was created on the Columbia because the style is evident.
Whether or not the others are native to this area is unknown as their distribution has never been analyzed.
Slave killers are much more common in California, but
there the usual style is slightly different from those found
locally, although the overall general motif is the same.

The single bladed club, second from the top in Fig.
52, is from the McLeod collection, and for symmetry and
finish is one of the finest ever found. It came from the
Oregon side of the river at the Long Narrows. The
double bladed one below it was found in the Cath-lah-
cum-up village (CO 3), on Sauvies Island, by Howard
Galbraith. Four others came from this place and as far
as I know are the only ones found an Sauvies Island, although a fragment came from the Cath-lah-min-na-min
site (CO 9), and a crude unfinished one made of a sliver

Fig. 53

UNUSUAL TYPE OF SLAVE KILLER

of basalt was found on the Cath-lah-nah-qui-ah village
(MU 6), also found by Howard Galbraith. The slave
killer on the bottom of Fig. 52 is from the Loftus collection, and has an unusual shape. It could well be that the
original head of this one was accidentally broken off and
the body refinished into the present form. It came from a
small island just above McNary Dam.

The superb specimen shown in Fig. 53 was found in a
prehistoric cremation pit on the Long Narrows, by Nola
St. Clair and Jim Leachman. Like the one from the John
Day River, it appears to be of local origin. The eye treat-

ment and the diamond pattern are characteristic, but the human hand outline is unique. I have never seen it on any other Columbia River sculpture. Cressman, in *Petroglyphs in Oregon*, lists handprints in but three sites in Oregon, and H. Thomas Cain, in *Petroglyphs of Central Washington*, shows them in only three places in Washington. Handprints, however, are quite common in other areas, notably in the Southwest.

The majority of clubs found are slate blades, twelve to sixteen inches long, double edged, and with a hole for a suspension thong. They would made fairly efficient weapons in battle, although easily broken, and that is what they may have been used for, although war between the Western Indians was quite rare. It is more likely that they were a show weapon like a sword worn by a modern officer. Every fisherman on the Columbia had a club with which to kill the salmon as soon as taken, lest this powerful fish escape. They were generally shaped of wood, or were even just a short stick. Sometimes these wooden clubs were carved, even in recent times. It is doubtful that the carved stone clubs were used for salmon killing; they were easily broken and required an enormous amount of work to fashion. Some very simple stone clubs, crudely pecked out of a sliver of basalt, have been found, they would have served very well for salmon killers.

Carved clubs of whalebone are occasionally found in cremations, and one or two plain ones have been found on the lower river. The carved specimens generally have a bird effigy handle, and were undoubtedly traded down from the Northwest coast. They are always badly shattered and burned. Complete prehistoric ones are practically non-existent on the river. The excellent specimen shown in Fig. 55 was found by Nola St. Clair and Jim Leachman, in the same cremation with the slave killer in Fig. 53. The carving is duplicated on the opposite side. One with a similar motif was found by the Harrisons on the John Day. A bird effigy handled club made of copper was found many years ago on the Deschutes River.

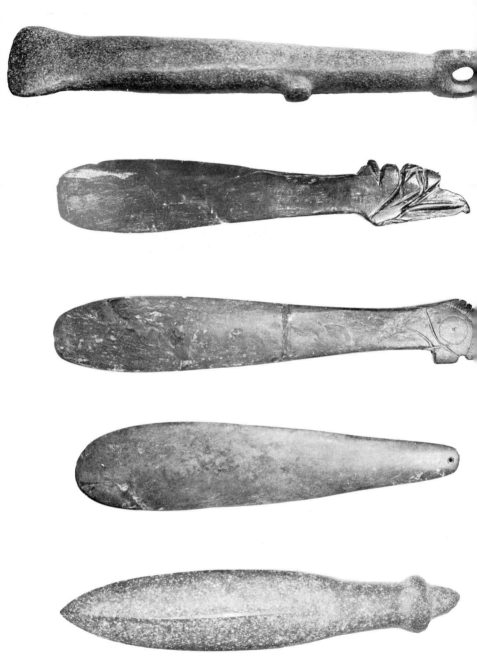

Fig. 54   **STONE CLUBS**

The club shown at the top of Fig. 54 is an especially interesting one. It is eighteen inches long and made of dense black basalt, highly polished. It has a chisel point

Fig. 55

WHALEBONE CLUB

instead of the usual blade, and the projecting knob is perplexing; it may have been a guard. It would have made a formidable weapon but would have taken an extremely strong man to wield it effectively. It was found on the Washington side of the Long Narrows by Frank Sauke.

Fig. 56

MONOLITHIC AXE

Next below it is a carved slate club from the Cowles collection. Below it is one of the Northwest Coast bird effigy clubs, found on the upper Columbia. The one below it is the most common type found along the river, a plain blade with a hole in the handle. These two are from the Jay Perry collection and are on display at the Sacajawea Museum in Pasco. In the bottom row is a granite club from the McLeod collection, found at Five Mile Locks. The blade is diamond shaped in cross section. The monolithic axe shown in Fig. 56 was found in a blown out grave near Alderdale, by Mr. E. R. Warner. It is somewhat similar to a type found in the eastern states and is probably not indigenous to the Columbia area. It is also on display at the Sacajawea Museum.

CHIPPED STONE

Chipped artifacts have a fascination for all collectors, and the Columbia has produced as fine specimens as are

Fig. 57

SCREENING FOR ARROW POINTS, DESCHUTES RIVER

found anywhere in the world. For delicacy and variety of forms and beauty of material they are unsurpassed. The river in cutting its gorge uncovered a variety of semiprecious gem material, agatized wood, jasper, rose quartz, moss agate and many others, all of which were utilized by the natives in fashioning their projectile points. Many are found in which the grain of the stone was utilized to give the finished product a gem-like effect, proving that they were fascinated by the beauty of the material and manipulated it to show the color to the best advantage.

Certain areas are noted for the class of points found, especially the mouth of the Deschutes River and Priest Rapids. The Deschutes enters the Columbia a few miles above Celilo, and is still a famous fishing stream. At its mouth was a village site covering several acres; through the centuries the sands built up ten or more feet, saturated with artifacts throughout its depth. High waters, notably the 1894 flood, highest on record, cut away this bank, dissolving away the sands and leaving the rocks and artifacts in a layer on the bedrock. During the early 1920s a crew of commercial diggers worked this layer for the arrow points which were sold to collectors in the east. One thousand points was considered a normal week's production, and of course, they kept only the very best, perfect ones. One digger recovered 600 points from an area only three feet square. Shortly before The Dalles Dam reservoir was filled, collectors started working the sands that had not been touched by the flood. The entire area was sifted to the bottom, as many as 75 screeners were counted there on one week end. The number of points recovered is unknown but it must have been many thousand, 25 per per person was an average day's work. All of them were of the finest workmanship and material, some of such delicate construction and beautiful stone that they should be classed as gems.

The Priest Rapids area is several miles long, the shifting sands and wandering river has eroded many of the camp sites, leaving a streak of gravel and artifacts, sometimes covered with four or more feet of blow sand. Collectors have worked this area for years, throwing off the sand and screening the rich gravel layer. The spaces between the boulders in a washed out site have also been productive. Many large collections were made from the Priest Rapids area.

The most exciting method of finding arrow points is surface hunting. Every spring the high waters uncover many points, the trick is to be the first one there, otherwise all you can find is tracks. Along the banks as the water goes down the chips and small stones collect in the little intercises in the clay and in the cracks in the bedrock. These must all be scratched out with a small hand cultivator or three tined rake, for that is where the points collect also. After the water recedes and the sands start to move in the wind, more are uncovered. But the best time is as the water goes down, and especially along the water's edge where the points show up clear and bright in the shallow water. One beautiful point picked up in this way produces more thrill than half a dozen in the screen; screening has a commercial quality about it that detracts from the pleasure, besides, it is hard work. While hunting the shore one has a chance to enjoy the companionship of the river and absorb a little of its romance.

The number of arrow points that have been picked up along the Columbia is unbelievable, a collector with less than 5,000 is considered just a dabbler. Ernest Cowles, a rancher from Grandview, during the depression of the 1930's when there was no market for fruit, picked up along the river and sold for ten cents each, over 10,000 of them, not counting the fine ones that he kept for himself. He has a wealth of other fine artifacts which he has found along the shores of the river, all housed in a special fire proof museum. Some men made their entire living hunting and selling arrow points.

The best known of the commercial diggers was Charles Beckman, familiarly known as Arrowhead Charley, a rugged individualist and worthy companion of the river.

Charley worked on the Celilo canal in 1915 and was fascinated by the many beautiful arrow points and other relics that turned up in the excavations, none of which the workmen were permitted to pick up. When the canal was finished Charley found out that arrow points could be sold, and spent his remaining 35 years in what to him was an absorbing way of life. He had a cabin at Roosevelt for his headquarters, but most of his time was spent on the river bank in some old Indian village.

Fig. 58

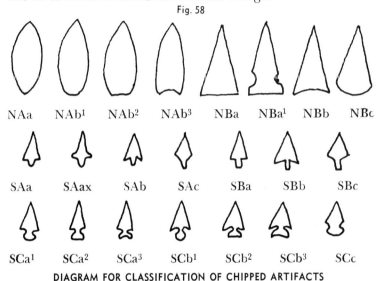

NAa NAb¹ NAb² NAb³ NBa NBa¹ NBb NBc

SAa SAax SAb SAc SBa SBb SBc

SCa¹ SCa² SCa³ SCb¹ SCb² SCb³ SCc

DIAGRAM FOR CLASSIFICATION OF CHIPPED ARTIFACTS

Charley had the utmost contempt for grave diggers; his method of hunting was that adopted by most subsequent collectors. Finding a village site that was all or partially washed away, he would dig down to the layer of gravel left behind as the silt and sand eroded, then rake the gravel into a small three sided screen with an open front and shake it out. Fifty points a day was the average take, once he got 15 in one screen. He recovered over 150,000 during his lifetime, besides a number of larger artifacts.

Whenever an exceptionally fine one would be found in the screen he would put it in his "good collection"

which he would not sell. "Some day," he said "I may
need some money and will sell them then, they are my
bank account."Shortly before he died he wrote Jay Perry
of Kennewick, saying that he needed money and was sending him his good collection of 350 points, every one a
work of art. They are now on display at the Sacajawea
Museum in Pasco, along with a large number he found
and sold to Mr. Charles Bassett, an industrialist of Buffalo, New York, who donated them to the museum as a
memorial to Charley.

There are several methods of classifying chipped artifacts, but that adapted by Gifford and Schenck is one of
the simplest. The points are divided into groups according to form; size is not a factor, as shown in Fig. 58. The
N means no stem. This type is generally a knife but some
of them may be spear heads or arrow points. Small triangular points are called war points, because having no
stem for hafting they would come off the shaft in a
wound. The S means stemmed. This chart is taken from
"Archaeology of The Dalles-Deschutes Region" and if
used and the source quoted, any archaeologist anywhere
will know what you are talking about. This classification
will cover all types of points except occasional freaks.

Most points classed as freaks are really reworked points.
One form often encountered has only one barb, the other
was broken off during manufacture or in service and that
side was rechipped into a point that was still usable. The
points called "stunners" are generally points that have
been reworked into scrapers or simply discarded when it
was found that they could not be rechipped into a serviceable point. The odd shaped points that are found are
more often the result of accident than design. To make
an arrow point is a relatively simple matter, an Indian
with ordinary skill could fashion one in five to ten minutes. To make the beautiful long symmetrical ones was of
course a different matter; they were made only by the
highly skilled and required much patience. Undoubtedly

many of these points broke just as the finishing touches were being put on.

The arrow point maker first found some suitable material, a piece of petrified wood, a flint nodule, or some agate for which the west is so famous. Then with a hammer stone made of an elongated river pebble a blow was struck on the edge of the material, breaking off a flake or spall. From a number of these flakes the worker selected those that had the proper form and thickness, and further fashioned them with light blows of the hammer stone; this is called percussion flaking and was the method used in making the most ancient tools used by man. After the piece was roughly shaped by percussion flaking it was held in one hand, perhaps with a bit of leather to protect the fingers from the sharp chips, and the point of a tool made from a piece of deer or elk horn (Fig. 88) was pressed against the edge, causing a small chip to fly off. This is called pressure flaking and was an important discovery by some long forgotten inventor. By working round and round with his flaking tool the maker gradually fashioned his point. The barbs and tang were put on last, the whole point finished to the individual taste with tiny chips along the edges, called secondary flaking.

One feature that most people find difficult to understand is that all chipping must be started from the edge, never from any other place. Those long chips that travel half way or perhaps all the way across, all were started from the edge of the piece. If a short stubby chip flies off it is impossible to start where it left off and continue. By skillful application of the tool the size and length of the chip could be controlled. Of course some material chips easier than others, and obsidian the best of all. The real artisan was one who could manipulate opal and some of the other semi-precious stones that lacked the chipping qualities of brittle material like obsidian. Some very fine points are made of basalt.

Unfortunately the white man has learned to chip stone

and has attained a skill equal to the best of the natives. Many of the long red, green or clear points found in curio shops, and some collections, had their start as a beer bottle or railroad signal light, both of which chip easily. All types of semi-precious stones are also used for fake points. Many eastern collectors refuse to take obsidian points, as faked ones are difficult to identify. Most of the others are readily spotted by the experienced, but if the unethical takes the time he can make a point that is impossible to tell from the genuine.

In many places along the Columbia the discarded spalls broken off in manufacturing arrow points lie a foot or more deep where the fine sand has drifted away leaving the heavier material behind. Fountain bar contains tons of them, and "rock hounds" are picking them up for gem material. Another good place, easily reached, is at the Maryhill ferry landing on the Washington side. Each spring flood uncovers a new supply of beautiful chips, and they can be found on every bar on the Columbia.

Some of the famed Columbia River arrow points are shown in Fig. 59. The four on the left in the top row are a special variety known as the basel-notched, a tiny notch is chipped in the center of the stem, this notch can also be seen in some other points in this picture. Although these four were found in the Atlatl Valley site, the center of their distribution seems to be the Priest Rapids area. Every point found with this notch is a masterpiece, a work of art in both form and material. It may have been the hallmark of an especially gifted craftsman. These four points were found together with five of the triangular "war points", two of which are shown on the right. Next to them is a special type with expanding body and ser-rated tangs found on Sauvies Island and vicinity; only five are known as far as I can determine. The one shown came from the Shoto village (CL 6) on Lake River, and was found by Dennis Strong. It is two and a quarter inches long. Large obsidian knives with the same type tang serrations have been found at the mouth of the John Day River.

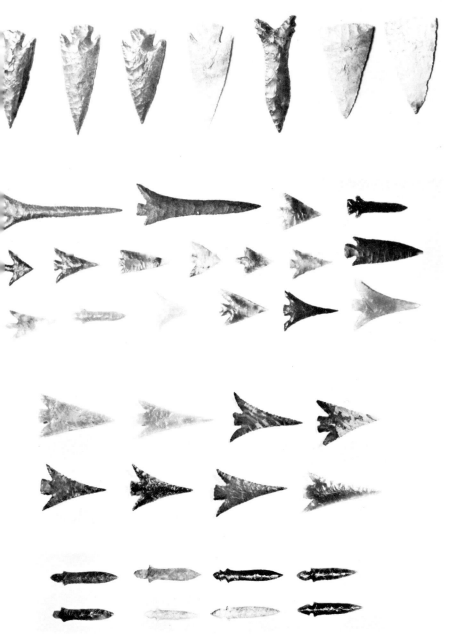

COLUMBIA RIVER GEM POINTS   Fig. 59

In the next two groups from the top are a few representative points from the area between the John Day and The Dalles. The long one in the upper left is of petrified wood, and is two and three-eighths inches long. Next to it is a basalt point and an especially fine one, although the maker had trouble with one barb. While the form of the arrow points shows in the picture, the beautiful material does not. Besides petrified wood and basalt, there are cornelian, jasper, opal, rose quartz, obsidian, moss agate, and other gem material. Note how many have the notched base.

The eight points on the bottom are the famed "dagger points" found at the Five Mile Lock site, and occasion-

Fig. 60

"MULE EAR" KNIVES

ally at other places. They are from one to one and a half inches long and were found by Elmer and Frank Buehler. The eight points above them came from the Morton collection.

One type of point, NAB3, Fig. 60, is called a "mule ear." It is found all along the river but is most common below the Cascades. It apparently was made to be hafted, in fact some have been found with the hafting in place. They occur in several different shapes, but they all started out formed about like the one third from the right. As it dulled in use and was resharpened, it assumed the shape of the one next to it, on the left, then the next, and after long use it might be almost entirely gone like the one on the extreme left.

The long thin points that are occasionally found, like the dagger type and the delicate ones in Fig. 59, were war

COLUMBIA RIVER KNIVES   Fig. 61

and show points; they were not used in hunting. Most of these came from burial grounds and are sometimes found in caches of three or four up to 25 or more. Some caches were excavated in Atlatl Valley: the points lay side by side, but were not all oriented in the same way so they could not have been attached to arrow shafts when placed in the grave, but instead were in a bag or pouch. These points were not worn as bangles or ornaments, as some believe; anyone who has used an arrow point for a tie clasp or other jewelry knows how shortly the brittle points and barbs will last. However, chipped pieces shaped similar to arrow points have been found in a position indicating use an ornament. The stem in this case will have a notch for the suspension cord.

Knives are found in two general types, NA and NB. Some are made to be hafted, and this is the most common type found in the old camps. Some have been found with part of the hafting still in place, where they were buried deep in the midden and protected from the elements. They average about two inches in length. The type NAa and NAb, made for use unhafted or used with the end wrapped with leather for a handle, is seldom found except in graves where it was the most common offering. These knives are four to seven inches long, averaging four and a half. Many are beautiful specimens. In one small cemetery near The Dalles over a thousand of them were found.

Fig. 61 shows some Columbia River knives. The three in the top row are typical although considerably finer specimens than usually found, and the type with the stem is rare. The one on the right is three and three-quarters inches long. Below them is a sixteen inch jasper knife found by Mr. A. J. Loftus, of Pasco, on a small island near Umatilla. Next is an obsidian blade found by Charles Hall on the Snake River just above Pasco. Blades as long as these are not common on the river. The stone knife in the bone handle was found by Howard Galbraith on Sauvies Island. Although not found *in situ*, the blade fits perfectly in the recess in the handle. Originally the blade was probably set with pitch and bound with leather or sinew.

Stone drills were used to bore holes in wood for the insertion of a thong for fastening. Thwarts were put in a canoe this way, and planks tied to a house. They were also used to drill bone and stone for beads, bangles, and pipes. There is some evidence that they were used hafted with a bow or spindle drill. It was a lot of work to penetrate stone or wood with these crude implements. One cannot but marvel at the patience displayed by the stone

Fig. 62

EFFIGIES

age artisans in forming his tools and utensils. Some drills have a tang like an arrow point. This was not done purposely so that it could be suspended from a cord for transporting, but simply because it was made from an arrow point.

Next to arrow points, scrapers are the most plentiful of chipped artifacts. Many are beautiful specimens and were one the handiest tools in an Indian village or camp.

They were used to dress down wooden implements, shape bone, scrape hides, and for many other chores. Even today an Indian woman prefers to dress deer skin with a stone scraper, Dr. David French of Reed College took a

Fig. 63

CHIPPED NOSE ORNAMENTS

picture of one working a hide with a stone scraper in a wooden handle, seated in the shade of her new Mercury sedan. Scrapers come in many shapes and sizes, some are merely a flake beveled on one side, while others are carefully shaped all around and tanged for a haft. One type is shaped like a thumb nail, it was used throughout the world. Scrapers were easily sharpened. Wooden artifacts found in the drowned village on Sauvies Island all show the marks of a flint scraper. A graver in a type of scraper with a sharp point used to incise wood, stone, or bone. They are not plentiful.

Chipped effigies like those in Fig. 62, are frequently encountered in curio shops and some collections; they are beautifully made because some white man made them to sell. The two shown here were found on old burial vault sites, but were found with trade goods so show white influence. The one in the upper left, of copper, and in the lower right, of red and black obsidian, were found together on Sullivan Island above Bonneville Dam. The other two came from Memaloose Island. The bird is black obsidian and the human figure is copper. These effigies were never made by prehistoric Indians.

The long chipped pieces shown in Fig. 63, are believed by amateurs to be nose ornaments. Early travelers tell of ornaments thrust through the nose although the only material mentioned is dentalium shell. One tribe of In-

Fig. 64

BANDED OBSIDIAN BLADE (Loftus Collection)

dians was called the Nez Percés, or Pierced Nose. These are all made of obsidian, the one with the sharpest curve is ground all over to prevent irritation. Straight ones cannot be told from drills unless they are ground down. Nose pieces were found in the Big Leap, Congdon, Maybe, and Bead Patch sites, all of which are considered to be quite old.

ARROWS AND ARROW MAKING

Arrow shafts were generally made of red cedar although other wood or straight reeds might be used. Cedar can be split into long straight pieces, dressed down with stone scrapers, then rounded and polished with a pair of shaft smoothers made of scorious lava or sandstone, generally the latter. Shaft smoothers are found throughout the Columbia River area. They are frequently beautifully made and many are found in pairs. The groove is circular but does not make a full circle when the faces are brought in

Fig. 65

ARROW SHAFT STRAIGHTENERS AND SMOOTHERS

contact; pressure could thus be brought to bear on the wood when dressing down the shaft. Another type of arrow smoother is made of dense smooth stone. These show evidence of heating and the use of oil; it is thought that they were heated and used to straighten out and perhaps harden the shaft. Two of this type are shown in Fig. 65. A stone shaped like a doughnut is considered by some to have been used to straighten arrows, the shaft was slipped through the hole and the stone twisted, bearing against the kink.The many shapes and sizes in which this stone is found make this use seem unlikely. In "Archaeology of the Upper Columbia," bone implements with a small hole in one end are called arrow wrenches.

In the prehistoric drowned village on Sauvies Island, arrow shafts are found, and Howard Galbraith found one with the stone point still attached although it had came apart in the screen. The end of the red cedar shaft was notched to receive the stem of the point, and bound in place with fiber. Pitch from pine trees was used to secure the binding although in this case the pitch had dissolved away. Sinew was generally used to bind the arrow to the shaft. Early writers always mention bone arrow points, evidently they were widely used although being subject to deterioration few are found except on the lower river where the soil is alkaline. The most usual type is about one inch or slightly longer, unbarbed, one end wedge shaped, the other tapering to a point, and about one-eighth inch in diameter at the largest part. The point of the three part fish spear is made in the same way, except that the butt-end is rounded instead of flattened. They look like small short awls.

Lewis and Clark describe arrows made in two parts. "Their bows are extremely neet and very elastic, they are about two feet six inches long and two inches wide in the center, thence tapering gradually to the extremities, where they are $3/4$ of an Inch wide, they are very flat and thin, formed of the heart of the arbor vita or white cedar, the back of the Bow being thickly covered with Sinues of the Elk laid on with a Gleue which they make from the Sturgeon; the String is made of the Sinues of the Elk also, the arrow is formed of two parts usually tho' Sometimes entire; those formed of 2 parts are unequilly devided, the part on which the feathers are placed occupie 4/5 of it's length and is formed of light white pine rather larger than a Swan's quill, in the lower extremity of this is a circular mortice Secured by sinues raped around it; this mortice receives the one end of the 2d part which is of smaller size than the first and about five inches long, in the end of this the barb is fixed and Confined with Sinues, the berb is either Iron Copper or Stone forming at its point a greater angle than those of any other Indians I have observed." They said this construction was to make the arrows float when used for hunting waterfowl. Arrows were carried in a side opening quiver made of skin, the side opening was more adaptable for use in a canoe than the top opening quiver favored by the Indians where horses were used.

While Alexander Henry was at the Cascades in 1814, attempting to retrieve a cargo of trade goods stolen by the Indians, a chief was captured as a hostage, Henry describes his arrows: "I had the curiosity to examine the quiver of arrows belonging to the prisoner. It was made of a black bear cub, and held 70 loose arrows, with a parcel of 10 more carefully tied with cedar bark. These last were examined minutely, and found to be poisened. Small strips of rattlesnake skin were stuck on the barbs by means of some glutinous substance which Casino told me was also poison. The arrows were neatly made of cedar, tipped with iron, and painted green, red, brown, and yellow. Some of the barbs are so loosly fixed in their sockets as to be left in the flesh they penetrate when the shaft is pulled out."

ATLATL WEIGHTS

The strange and beautiful stones shown in Fig. 66 are considered to be atlatl weights, although there is as yet

0   1   2   3
INCH

ATLATL WEIGHTS   Fig. 66

no positive proof that they were. They are similar to stones found in other parts of the United States that have been found *in situ* and known to be so used. The atlatl is a device used for throwing a dart. It is a stick about 18 inches long with a handle at one end and a hook at the other for engaging the butt of the dart. The thrower is held over the shoulder paralled to the ground, with the dart held in place with the fingers. With an overhand throw the dart is hurled with great velocity, the thrower or atlatl acting as an extension to the wielder's arm. This device is known throughout the world. It is supposed to have preceded the invention of the bow and arrow. Being a weapon used in war and hunting, it eventually become a symbol of rank and influence, and was often highly decorated and frequently used as a grave offering.

The only early historian that mentions the atlatl along the Columbia is Robert Stuart, one of the original Astor overland party, who says "The boards used in throwing these darts are very judiciously fixed, in semblance of a gutter, which enables the natives to cast them with great exactness to a considerable distance." The natives he saw using the atlatl were Aleut or perhaps Northern Tlingit hunters brought down by the Russian or other fur traders. There is no evidence that the atlatl was used by local natives in late times. Lewis and Clark, Henry, Franchére, and others who describe the natives and their habits in great detail, do not mention the atlatl, which they certainly would have if observed. Atlatls were found by Dr. Cressman in the high desert country of Southeastern Oregon, and weights similar to the long one with the notches in the end shown in Fig. 66 are also found there. Atlatl spurs or hooks were found in the Roadcut site at Five Mile Locks, but these were several thousands years older than the stone weights as proven by the chipped points found in association with them.

These weights are found in small numbers all along the river, but the greatest concentration of them was in The Dalles area. About 150 were found in the Atlatl Valley site, and a number in the Congdon, Big Leap, and Maybe sites. A large percentage of them were found in pairs. There are three general types. Shown at the top of Fig. 66 is the most common kind, a notched stone weighing from one and a half to 10 ounces. It is frequently decorated with grooved lines and nearly always shows careful workmanship and high polishing. The bottom is slightly convex. They are always made of highly colored stone, the one on the left is a catlanite, a bright red stone from the plains where it was used for making pipes. Spotted porphyry, quartz, colored granite, and other stone were used also.

The drilled weights shown in the second row from the top are generally made of galena, a lead ore, although a few have been found made of stone. The bottom of this type is flat, and they do not vary so greatly in size as those made of stone. The galena ones are always badly corroded. On the right is a galena weight, on the left, drilled stone. The third type is a long slim stone, somewhat flat on the bottom, with a notch in each end for the cord tie. Some of these are decorated with incised lines. On the bottom of Fig. 66 is a carved weight; this one and fragments of two others are the only ones of this type found along the river. It is made of dense hard black stone. The weights shown are from the Bergen, McLeod, Selby, and Cowles collections, reading top to bottom. The scale applies to the bottom one only.

Experiments by various amateurs have shown that the attachment of a weight to an atlatl serves no useful purpose, and the heavy ones seem to be definitely detrimental to the accuracy of the throw. It is thought that they were used as a charm, rather than to obtain improved performance, if indeed they were atlatl weights. It is definite that they were tied to something, and the use of galena, a very heavy ore, suggests their use as weights. Since, when found in pairs, they were often far from equal in weight, their use as counterbalances or flyweights on, for instance, a drill, seems highly improbable. They may have had some unknown use, such as a game. Many of the stone weights are badly scarred on the bottom. But they are known as atlatl weights to all, so are called that here, but there still is no proof that they were used for that purpose.

WEDGES AND MAULS

Wedges made of wood, bone, and horn were used for splitting wood, felling trees, and making house planks and canoes. Stone wedges may have also been used but if so were not struck with a maul, they served to follow up the crack made by the driven wedges. The instrument used to drive them was a bottle shaped pestle made of stone,

Fig. 67

WOOD, BONE AND HORN WEDGES

or even a river pebble held in the hand. Hammers made for use with a handle were not used, the girdled stone objects commonly called hammers by collectors were net sinkers; fiber was wrapped around the groove and the pit in the groove served to insert the rope under the wrapping to tie it to the net. Girdled stones were hafted in the Northwest coast and also in the plains, some of them may have been used along the river, but if so they were late in arriving, and their use limited. The girdled stones are found in large numbers along the lower river. If they had been used hafted in any quantity broken ones would be found, just as so many pieces of hand mauls are picked up in the old villages; but when a broken girdled stone is found it is generally from being used as a cooking stone. It has been said that they were hammers because they are found so far from the river at times; too far to be sinkers but could have been a hammer lost while cutting a tree. But just where the river was a few hundred years ago, no one knows. Where the stone was found may have been the river or slough bank when it was lost. Round river pebbles were used for hammers as well as the carved stone mauls, and a girdled net weight could have been used the same way. None of the early writers mention hafted hammers, although all other habits of the natives were described in great detail. War clubs with wooden handles were used, however.

Bone and antler wedges are common in the village sites below the Cascades. Saturated with oil from handling, they last for centuries in the non-acid soil (bone decays rapidly if the soil is acid). On the upper river they deteriorate rapidly, and few are found although they were very important. The only source of fuel was driftwood, which required splitting before use. In the forested region west of the Cascades, after a few decades all the wood near a village would be used and the natives would then use driftwood. The favorite fuel, however, was fir bark. After a large fir tree dies the bark becomes loose and finally it all slides to the ground, several cords of the finest fuel. Bark burns with a hot, smokeless flame. In the old camp sites there are deep beds of the ashes of fir bark. Elkhorn pri-bars were used to remove the bark from down timber, and it may be that a hafted tool something like a pick was used to break up the bark into useful lengths. This fuel could be transported a considerable distance either in canoes or on the backs of the women.

Lieutenant Clark stopped at an Indian lodge near the mouth of the Yakima River, observing, "I entered and found it crouded with men, women and children and near the entrance of these houses I saw many squars engaged splitting and drying Salmon. I was furnished with a mat to set on, and one man set about prepareing me something to eate, first he brought in a pece of a Drift log of pine and with a wedge of the elks horn and a malet of Stone curioesly carved he Split the log into Small pieces and lay'd it open on the fire on which he put round stones, a woman handed him a basket of water and a large Salmon about half dried, when the stones were hot he

Fig. 68

STONE MAULS

put them into the basket of water with the fish which was soon boiled sufficiently for use, it was taken out put on a platter of rushes neetly made, and set before me." This was in 1805. The natives there had never seen a white man and were as yet uninfluenced by them. This domestic scene was typical in camps and villages all up and down the river, and probably had not changed for centuries. Cooking was women's work, but men always did the cooking for visitors.

Horn and bone wedges were made by cutting off a section with a stone knife, then grinding the material down on a sandstone slab. Hundreds of bone and antler fragments are found on the lower river showing these cuts; antlers are frequently found with all the prongs cut off. Sandstone slabs are picked up with deep grooves worn in them from making wedges, the groove is the same width as the wedge. Bone wedges are quite rare but those made of antler are common, the head end, battered by hammering, has generally deteriorated.

Wood wedges are extensively used but are never found except where constant immersion in water has preserved them, as in the drowned village on Sauvies Island. They were made of hemlock knots and various hard woods. The tops were tightly bound with split willow wythes to prevent shattering under the blows of the stone hammer. Lewis and Clark mention them: "The wood of this tree is excessively hard when seasoned. The Natives make great use of it to form their wedges of which they split their boards of Pine for the purpose of building houses. Those wedges they employ in common with those formed of the Elks horn, in Splitting their fire wood and in hollowing out their canoes. I have seen the natives drive the wedges of this wood into a solid dry pine which it cleft without fractureing or injuring the wedge in the smallest degree."

Horn, bone, and wood wedges from the Lynn Woodcock collection are shown in Fig. 67. Those in the top row are elkhorn and are typical, they are beveled on one side and the point is rounded or almost square. The bone wedges, shown below, always have the tapering point. The wood wedge is made of a hemlock limb and was found in the drowned village. The wrapping on the driving end is shown. Nearly all wooden wedges found have the point broken off.

Hand mauls, Fig. 68, are found all along the river.

This tool is often highly embellished and polished, especially those from the upper river. It was a favorite grave offering. After the 1948 flood Guy Gilbert, of Kennewick, nearly swamped his boat with a load of them he picked up on a small island just below the mouth of the Snake River. The material used for making mauls was generally dense basalt, but granite, quartzite, and other hard stone was also used. The mallet was held in one hand and swung endways, striking with the butt, it could deliver a hard blow. A few abrasions on the sides of some show that they were occasionally used similar to a sculptor's mallet, an object of the same shape. Some of the most highly decorated mauls show no marks of use; they were evidently an object for show or ceremonial use only. In many museums mauls are labeled "pestles" and it is common to see a bowl with a maul in it as a bowl-pestle combination. They may have been used occasionally as pestles but their primary function was for driving.

The maul on the left of Fig. 68, is from the Maybe site. It has a bird effigy handle. The one in the center is also basalt, highly polished, and came from the Pasco vicinity. The one on the right was found at the mouth of the John Day River, and the handle is a perfect turtle when viewed from the top. These are from the Bergen, Morton, and Harrison collections, respectively.

ADZE BLADES

The Indians along the Columbia had no axes. Instead, they felled their trees and worked their wood with the adze. It was their one indispensable tool and is still used, although now the blades are steel. Precontact adze blades were made of bone, shell, or stone. The blade was lashed to a wood or bone handle in such a manner that it could be drawn toward the worker when making a stroke, the worker thus had complete control over the tool. Lewis and Clark describe the use of the adze: "the only tool usually imployed in felling the trees or forming the canoe carving &c is a chissel formed of an old file about one inch or Inch and a half broad. This chissel has sometimes a large block of wood for a handle; they grasp the chissel just below the block with the right hand holding the edge down while with the left they take hold of the top of the

Fig. 69

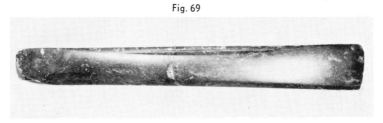

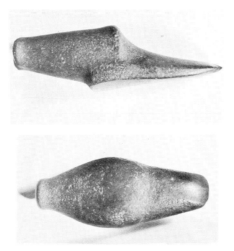

STONE ADZES

block and strike bachanded against the wood with the edge of the chissel. a person would suppose that the forming of a large canoe with an instrument like this was the work of several years, but these people make them in a few weeks." The stone adze or "chissel" was used in this manner for centuries before the white invasion. Various types of adze handles are shown in Ronald Olson's *Adze, Canoe, and House Types of the Northwest Coast.*

Adze blades are found throughout the length of the

Columbia but the longest and best are found on the up-per river. In length they range from one to sixteen inches.

Fig. 70

BONE ADZE HANDLE, SAUVIES ISLAND

The stone most commonly used is jadite, but serpentine, nephrite, basalt, and other materials were also used. Jadite is found in the vicinity of the Fraser and Rogue Rivers. It is a beautiful green stone and takes a high polish and sharp edge. Blocks are sometimes found that show the method of cutting. It can also be seen on the edges of some blades such as the long one in Fig. 69. The stone was cut with a thin sandstone slab that was drawn back and forth across the cut, in the presence of water. After the notch was sufficiently deep the stone was broken the rest of the way and the rough edges ground down. The blade is commonly called a celt and is found throughout the United States. It was frequently used as a grave offering.

In Fig. 69, top, is shown a sixteen inch adze blade found on the upper river by Jay Perry; it is now in the Sacajawea Museum. In the center is an excellent example of a monolithic adze, a type comparatively rare on the Columbia. It is from the Cowles collection. The handle was grasped in one hand and the other used to guide the blade, as Lewis and Clark described the use of the chisel with the wood block handle.

The tool shown at the bottom of Fig. 69 is from the Sams collection. It is usually called a stone wedge by collectors but actually is another form of monolithic adze. Ronald Olson in *Adze, Canoe, and House Types of the Northwest Coast,* says about this type: "From the valleys of the Columbia and Fraser are some few archaeological specimens which are quite different from those used in historic times. Those from the Columbia are pestle-shaped stones with handle and cutting edge in one piece."

Fig. 70 shows a bone adze blade handle from Sauvies Island. There is a recess in the end for insertion of the blade.

BOWLS AND PESTLES

Stone bowls and pestles are the most well known of all

artifacts except arrow points and need little explanation. Bowls are not too plentiful on the river because the natives used wood for this service more than stone, and the wood of course has disappeared. Lewis and Clark write: "The Culinary articles of the Indians in our neighborhood (Clatsop) consist of wooden bowls and throughs, baskets, wooden spoons and woden scures or spits. Their wooden bowls and troughs are of different forms and sizes, and most generally dug out of a solid piece; they are ither round or semi- globular, in the form of a canoe, cubic, and cubic at top terminating in a globe at the bottom; these are extremely well executed and many of them neatly carved, the larger vessels with hand-holes to them; in these vessels they boil their fish or flesh by means of hot stones which they immerce in the water with the article to be boiled. they also render the oil of fish or other anamals in the same manner." Stone bowls are found in the area between the Kalama River and the John Day. Below the Kalama, wood was the favorite material for all artifacts; while above the John Day the nomadic life of the natives made heavy stone implements impractical. Stone bowls were used even in modern times. Before The Dalles Dam drowned out the Long Narrows and Celilo, they were often seen in use there, as were stone pestles. Wooden and stone bowls are still used on some reservations.

All small bowls are called paint pots by most collectors, but many of them could not have been used for the purpose of grinding and mixing paint. Some are of porous lava which would have trapped the paint, and some are much too deep for convenience. All dishes still bearing the marks of paint are flat and shallow like a saucer, some have as many as five depressions, each with a different color paint. Small bowls are frequently decorated, it is probable that they were used by the shaman for mixing his herbs and potions.

Pestles are one of the most common artifacts on the river. A great many of them show little workmanship,

STONE BOWLS FROM THE COLUMBIA RIVER   Fig. 71

being a natural shaped stone with some pecking to improve the form. Most of them are cylindrical and tapered, although occasionally a square one is found. The difference between a pestle and a maul has already been explained. Pestles sometimes measure nearly 30 inches long; if over about 20 inches, they are called "salmon packers," on the supposition that they were used to pack dried and shredded salmon into the long storage bags. This is highly unlikely, the good ones show very little use, and they are found in areas where salmon was not preserved as it was on the upper Columbia. A wood pestle would have been

Fig. 72

WOOD BOWLS

a much more practical instrument. The long pestles are beautifully worked and shaped. Long pestles, like all implements for which the use is unknown, have been designated as "ceremonials." The reason why so many pestles are found and so few bowls, is that the stone pestles were used with wooden bowls. Stone bowls were used for cooking by the hot stone boiling method.

Stone bowls were made by the pecking process, the hollow was pecked out first then the exterior finished. Pestles were made of a sliver of basalt or a long river pebble. The stone was placed on a layer of sand or soil to act as a cushion during the pecking process. Especially fine pestles were polished with sand and water.

In Fig. 71, are shown some of the finer examples of carved stone bowls from the Columbia. The one on the upper left is about 14 inches in diameter with an especially pleasing decorative motif. It was found by Herbert Veason on the Long Narrows. On the upper right is a bowl found by Carrel Morton in the Congdon site. This

Fig. 73

(Cowles collection)

"SALMON PACKING" PESTLES, COLUMBIA RIVER
The one in the center is 29 inches long and has a snake carved in relief on each side.

type of bowl, rare on the river, is common in California. A similar one, somewhat smaller, came from the Maybe site. The zoomorphic bowl in the lower left is made of granite and is nine inches in diameter. It is, for perfection of form and style, one of the best ever found on the river. It washed out of a gravel bank near Wishram after the pool behind The Dalles dam was filled. The stylized bowl in the lower right is from the Arch M. Sams collection and was found near Prindle, a few miles below the Cascades.

The wooden bowl on the left in Fig. 72 may not be prehistoric; its age is unknown but it is similar to those described by the early writers. It is owned by Frank Wilke. The "trough" on the right is prehistoric, it was found in the drowned village on Sauvies Island by Leon Tabor. It is made of cedar, carved with stone and bone tools. A piece of the rim has been broken off and repaired by drilling holes and lacing the broken piece down.

DIGGING TOOLS

The implement used by the prehistoric natives in digging roots, which formed a considerable portion of their food supply, was a slightly curved stick about four feet long, sharpened at one end and hardened in the fire. Sometimes the working end was shod with a horn or flint point. On the upper end, like the D handle on a shovel, was fitted a cross piece of wood bound with sinew, or a piece of elkhorn drilled to received the top of the stick. Again Lewis and Clark observed: "The instruments used by the natives in digging their roots is a strong stick of three and a half feet long Sharpened at the lower end

Fig. 74

ANTLER DIGGING STICK HANDLE

and at its upper inserted a part of an Elks or bucks horn which Serves as a handle, standing transvirsely on the stick." A similar instrument is still used; in 1956 I saw an Indian woman digging roots with a stick to which was lashed a wooden cross piece, working in a swamp near the Long Narrows. And again, one at Celilo was seen digging roots "for medicine for a sick boy," with a similar tool. Some of these tools were made of an iron rod, slightly curved. The stick handle shown in Fig. 74. was found on Sauvies Island, and is eight inches long. The hole is rectangular; eliptical holes were used by some of the tribes. It is said that a digging stick handle was made for a young girl when she was first able to help with the food gathering, and that she kept it all her life, and when she died it was buried with her.

The partially worked basalt slabs shown in Fig. 75 are

digging tools. Some of them have formed handles and
rather well chipped working surfaces; many are natural
flakes with a minimum of dressing. Another type is an
elongated river pebble with one end beveled by percussion flaking. It is likely that they were used for many
other purposes besides digging. They would have been
useful for removing and breaking bark for fuel, scraping

Fig. 75

(Sams collection)

BASALT SLAB DIGGING TOOLS

away charcoal when burning down a tree, or for hollowing out a canoe, even for breaking bones to extract the
marrow. A few have been found with the edge ground
down sharp. They are plentiful on the old camp sites, but
many do not recognize them for the useful tools that
they were.

POLISHED SCRAPERS

The implements shown in Fig. 76 are polished scrapers, made by percussion flaking a flat river pebble
all the way around, then grinding it to a sharp edge.

Many are beautiful specimens, symmetrically formed of dark, fine grained stone. highly polished, which may have been the result of long use. Their specific use is unknown but most amateurs believe they were a hide dressing tool. Hides were tanned by soaking them in warm water and deer brains, alternately soaking and drying the hide until it was cured. Holes were punched along the edges and the hide stretched by lacing it to a framework. Then with a stone or bone tool the hide was vigorously rubbed. As the hide stretched from working, the thongs were tight-

Fig. 76

POLISHED SCRAPERS

ened, and in this way the skin could be dressed down to the. thickness desired. After rubbing, the hides were smoked over a fire of rotted wood by placing it on a frame made of willow twigs over a pit enclosing the fire.

The artifact on the right in Fig. 76 is an unusual piece, it is four inches long and on one side is a rest for the thumb and for the fingers on the opposite side. The straight edge is very much worn and polished. It may be a tool for rubbing hides but it could also have been a bark breaker. Cedar bark was one of the most useful materials the Western Indians possessed. From it they made mats, baskets, rope, clothing, and many other useful things. From the bark, after stripping it from the tree, the dark smooth inner layer was removed and split into fibers, used without further work for making rope or mats. If for clothing or padding for infants' cradles, the bark was laid crosswise over a smooth pole and shredded by beating it with a smooth faced tool. It could be shredded almost as fine as cotton, and in this state was used for padding, towels, fire tinder, wrapping valuables (see the padding in the Chief Moses pipe case, Fig. 50), and head bands. For clothing it was spun into coarse threads by rolling on the thigh, the threads were then woven onto a belt, making a sort of grass skirt which, according to Ross, "might deserve praise for its simplicity, or rather for oddity, but it does not screen nature from the prying eye; yet it is remarkably convenient on many occasions. In a calm the sails lie close to the mast, metaphorically speaking, but when the wind blows the bare poles are seen."

COBBLE CHOPPERS

In *Archaeology of The Dalles-Deschutes Region* these chipped pieces, Fig. 77, are called "throwing stones" but are now generally called cobble choppers. It is extremely unlikely that they were used for throwing as a weapon. In *Archaeology of the Upper Columbia Region* they are

Fig. 77

COBBLE CHOPPERS

called discoidal scrapers. I have never seen in any discussion a statement as to their specific use. It is likely that they were a general purpose tool; they would have made an ideal implement for shredding salmon after it had been dried and was being made into pemmican.

They are made of a piece of river gravel, percussion flaked generally all the way around but sometimes only part way. They vary in size from one inch in diameter up to five inches, most are about two or two and a half. They were found in great numbers in the vicinity of the Long Narrows and Celilo. In the Big Leap site a cache of 150 of them was uncovered, and several containing a dozen or so up to 35 or 50. They decrease in number each way from Celilo but are still found in quantity as far as the John Day River and down to the Bead Patch site. Below the Cascades they are not found. This would indicate that they were used in preparing dried salmon, for west of the mountains the climate did not permit the curing of the salmon as did the dry, hot region to the east.

WAR CLUB HEADS

The Columbia River Indians, like those throughout the world, had stone war club heads, made to be used with a wooden handle. In the old camps, stones fashioned into globular or prismoidal forms are sometimes found. They may also be weapons, made to be enclosed in a buckskin sack on the end of handle. Most of the banded type come from the Long Narrows-Celilo region but they are found

Fig. 78

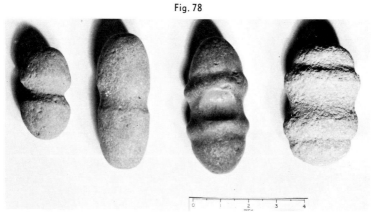

STONE WAR CLUB HEADS

all along the river. They vary in size, the longest are about nine inches but the average is three or four. Occasionally one is carved, and nearly all are nicely shaped and finished. One type, second from the right in Fig. 78, has a socket for the end of the handle.

FISHING TOOLS

Since fishing was the most important prehistoric industry it is natural that the tools used for this purpose would be the most plentiful of all artifacts found along the river, except arrow points which were easily made and considered expendable. All of the nets, weirs, harpoons, spears, floats and other wooden and fiber implements are of

Fig. 79

TYPES OF NET SINKERS

course gone, but some of the bone points and all of the stone tools still exist somewhere near or under the river. Until a few years ago banded and notched sinkers were casually overlooked; while hunting the shores a collector could overload himself before lunch time, but now they are all being picked up.

Net sinkers occur in a great variety of forms that are divisible into three types: banded, perforated, and notched. On the lower river, below the Long Narrows, the banded sinker is the most common. It was formed of a river pebble weighing a pound or more, around the center a notch was pecked to hold the cord by which it was suspended from the net. Most of them have a pit cut into the notch which served to permit insertion of the suspension cord beneath the fiber wrapped around the notch. It was the work of but a few minutes to make an ordinary banded sinker satisfactory for the purpose, but many were worked into attractive and symmetrical shapes. Some were cut into perfect rectangular blocks before banding, and others were decorated with incised lines or pecked ridges and rings. Above each sinker on the net was a wooden float to hold the net upright. James G. Swan says, "Peculiarly shaped sticks of dry cedar are used for floats, and the weights at the bottom are river pebbles of about a pound each, notched to keep them from slipping from their fastenings, and securely held by withes of cedar firmly twisted and woven into the foot rope of the net."

Perforated sinkers occur in a variety of forms but the most common is a flat river pebble, unworked except for a hole pecked through from each side. The hole is commonly near the center but may be on one edge. A few have been found with two holes. Soft sedimentary or volcanic rock was generally used as it was easy to perforate. This was done by pecking with a hammerstone of hard material like quartzite. Perforated sinkers on the lower river sometimes are found in caches of from two or three to as many as 44, found by the late Robert Miller on the shore where the Vancouver Shipyards was later built. On Lake River the receding flood waters once left seven of them stacked up on the bank like dinner plates. The cache shown in Fig. 3 was dug out of the clay after one was washed out by the waters. These caches are not in graves but simply where the fisherman buried them for safety at the close of the fishing season. Banded sinkers are seldom found in caches. They probably were not considered as valuable as the perforated ones. Another type of perforated sinker has an oblong hole that was made by grinding. They are found in what appear to be the older sites. Most of them are considerably larger than the usual perforated sinker.

Perforated sinkers are occasionally decorated; a few look like pendants and show considerable skill and endeavor in carving. These may have been used at the end of the net as a charm. In Fig. 80 are shown some carved sinkers found at the Cascades by Arch M. Sams.

Fig. 80

CARVED NET SINKERS

(Sams collection)

The notched sinker is simply a small flat river pebble with one, two, or four notches formed by percussion flaking. They are one of the most common rocks found on the river, and apparently were made as needed, and not saved and stored away for future use as were the banded and perforated sinkers.

By far the most banded and perforated sinkers are found in the area between the Kalama River and the Cascades. At certain favorite seining places, such as the stretch above the Short Narrows, near White Salmon and Klickitat Rivers, and the "Pump House" site near Crates Point, they are found in quantity. But below the Cascades they occur everywhere. Above the Long Narrows the banded sinkers show very little workmanship, and perforated ones are rare. Single notched sinkers are found below The Dalles. Between the Long Narrows and the John Day River most of them are two-notched, while above, the four-notched predominates.

The nets used by the natives were made of a sort of linen made of nettles, or of Indian Hemp, or spruce roots. Sometimes they were made very large, a hundred feet long and six feet wide. Nets were cast from a canoe as it was paddled along, then brought ashore by a line. One

Fig. 81

STONE AND BONE NET GAUGES

cast of the net might catch a hundred salmon. Below the Cascades, practically all fishing on the river was with the net. Skimming nets, formed on a loop of some pliable wood like vine maple, about four feet in diameter, and with a fir handle twelve or more feet in length, were used in the eddys and backwaters of the rapids for dipping up the fish. Adaptations of the skimming net were used for smelt and other small fish on the lower river. To gauge the mesh while weaving the net the implement shown in Fig. 81 was used. Some of these implements were made of bone. Wood was the most common material, but those now found are nearly all made of stone. They are quite rare, although the wood ones were plentiful in the old villages. Spier and Sapir say, "Gauges were used in fabricating all nets. These were flat slabs of elkhorn, a quarter inch or more in thickness, three or four inches long, and of various widths. A width of one-half inch was suitable for the mesh of eel nets, two and a half to three inches for steelhead, blueback, and silver salmon, three to four inches for chinook and sturgeon." The gauge on the bottom of Fig. 81 is of elkhorn and was found on Sauvies

Fig. 82

BONE HARPOONS

Island; the other is of stone and was found in the Indian Well site.

The most comon type of bone harpoon used in fishing was made of three parts, shown in Fig. 88, No. 6. The two collars were fitted around the bone point and bound together to a cord about a foot long, which was fastened to the pole. The ends of the collars opposite the point flare out for barbs, and the space between is hollowed out to receive the rounded end of the pole. This spear was thrust, not thrown, and when a fish was impaled the harpoon slipped off the pole and was held by the cord, thus preventing the struggles of the fish from breaking the pole. This instrument is found all along the river, many were found in Wakemap Mound.

Fig. 82 shows some of the conventional type harpoon points. The one on the top, from the Hall collection, and the next below, from the Morton collection, were found in Wakemap Mound. The bottom one was found in site CO 7 on Sauvies Island. It has a lateral line guard, a type rare along the river.

The stone sinkers in Fig. 79 are, left to right, single notch, double notch, four notch, banded, and perforated; the one on the right is a fairly rare type found only above The Dalles and generally considered to be canoe anchors as they are always large and heavy. Sometimes canoe anchors were perforated. I have one that is 16 inches in diameter and weighs 35 pounds. Banded sinkers that weigh several pounds were probably canoe anchors. Canoes were seldom anchored, they were always drawn up on the shore if at all possible. On the upper river the very high winds that sweep upstream cause high waves. If the canoes could not be brought ashore it would have been necessary to anchor them out in the stream where they would not be injured.

Modern informants say that fishing stations at such favorite locations as the Cascades, Long Narrows and Celilo were individually or family owned, and passed on by inheritance. They were highly prized, for the rugged,

steep rock walls left few places convenient for fishing the
violent waters, although there were many places where

Fig. 83

SALMON CARVED FROM ELK HORN

(Tabor collection)

fish could be taken. But certain places were much better
than others, where the currents set so the fish swam close
to a large rock in an eddy, or where they passed through

Fig. 84

(Seufert collection, Oregon Historical Society)

INDIAN FISHING CAMP ON THE LONG NARROWS, ABOUT 1895

a narrow channel. Since the water at the Long Narrows rises 45 feet or more during the spring high water, and Celilo Falls disappears during the flood season, several stations, or levels, were required depending on the stages of the river. Platforms were erected, where the terrain permitted, by setting posts in the bottom when the water was low, to which poles were tied to form a base for the platform.

The fish belonged to the fisherman and his family but custom permitted the old people, and possibly anyone who wanted them, to take the fish that they needed from the catch as the fisherman killed them and removed them from his net, casting them in a pile behind him. But if he wanted to keep all of his catch he would say so by slapping his buttocks; words could not be heard above the roar of the river.

On the upper river fish traps were used. On the small streams weirs were made by inserting willow poles across the stream with a narrow gate leading into the trap. At some falls a basket trap was used. As the heavy fish leap the falls they frequently fail to jump high enough to reach the crest and fall back; the baskets were set so the fish would fall into them, and they could not escape. This method was used at Kettle Falls, where all the fish belonged to the chief but were distributed free to all of the tribe.

MAT MAKING

Two of the most useful furnishings of an Indian lodge were mats and baskets. No family could have too many mats. They were extensively used for floor covering, bedding, partitions, for nearly everything for which we would use cloth. On the upper river the houses were made of them, and sometimes on the lower river they were used for temporary shelters. Small mats were used for plates and platters. Mat making was one of the principal duties of the Indian women.

The ordinary cat-tail rush was generally used to make the mats. The reed was cut during the summer, dried in the sun, and stored away until the rainy winter season kept the natives indoors. The rushes were sorted and cut to length, then laid side by side with the large and small ends alternating. The stalks were sewn together with a

Fig. 85

MAT CREASER

long slim needle made of wood or bone, and fiber cord. After withdrawing the needle an instrument called a mat creaser was passed over the seam. The seams were about four inches apart. The mat, after sewing, was bound all around with braid. Sleeping mats were about six feet long, and those used for lining the houses were from ten to twenty feet in length.

James Swan in *The Northwest Coast* says about mats: "Some are very prettily ornamented around the edges with colored grasses, neatly worked and woven in. These mats are so well made that they shed water like a duck's back, and, when set on their edge, as effectively exclude rain as the best shingle roof. The newly-made ones have a very fragrant smell, which makes them pleasant and healthy to sleep upon."

The mat creaser was a crescent shaped piece of wood or bone with a handle, often highly carved. Along the bottom was a groove which was passed over the seam, breaking over the fibers to prevent them from splitting.

The one shown in Fig. 85 is made of cedar and was found on the drowned village site on Sauvies Island by Lynn Woodcock. It is prehistoric, shaped and carved with stone and bone tools. It has the exposed rib motif in the characteristic Columbia River art style.

ABRASIVE STONES

In prehistoric times wood was carved with stone and bone tools and by means of controlled fire. These methods normally left an uneven surface and for the final finishing several forms of abrasive stones were used. They occur in considerable numbers in the old camp sites. Scorious

Fig. 86

ABRASIVE STONES

lava was the most used stone for wood, as it cuts rapidly. This material was formed from molten lava that was full of gas; when released from pressure the gas expanded, forming millions of bubbles which leave a sharp edge when the rock is broken. It occurs in many forms, from extremely rough to a fine grained stone.

Abrasive stones were used for other materials besides wood. It was about the only way bone and antler could be fashioned into needles, awls, wedges, and the many other useful products. Rubbing stones have been found with grooves in them that just fit needles and wedges, like the one illustrated in the lower left of Fig. 86. The stone in the upper left was used for polishing beads, it was found in the Maybe site with beads that fit the grooves. It is a fine grained sandstone. The light colored stone in the bottom row is pumice, used for the final polishing on bone. Abrasive stones with scalloped edges like the one shown are sometimes found. Evidence of paint on some suggests that they were used to grind paint from a slab, but they might have been painted for ornamental purposes.

Abrasive stones were also used to saw up slabs of steatite or jadite to make ornaments, pipes, and adze blades.

DENTALIA SHELLS

Dentalium played such an important part in the economy of the Columbia River Indians that it is deserving of considerable detail. By means of this small insignificant shell and the slave traffic, the Chinooks became wealthy, trading shell for slaves at the great trade mart at the Long Narrows, and slaves for shell with the North Coast tribes. Before the beaver became the standard of value as a result of the white invasion, the dentalium was the medium of exchange, valued according to length.

The shell is tapered like an elephant's tusk, slightly curved, one eighth or a bit more in diameter at the large end. It occurs in various lengths up to nearly three inches, but averages from one to one and a half inches. It grows mainly in the sea off the coast of Vancouver Island in fairly deep water. A few would occasionally wash ashore, but fishing was the only practical method of obtaining them in any quantity. Modern informants say that the instrument used in gathering them was a bundle of cedar

splints attached to a handle, something like a broom.
Over this was slipped a board with a hole of the proper
size to compress the splints, weighted down with stones.
Standing in a canoe the fisherman thrust down the pole,

Fig. 87

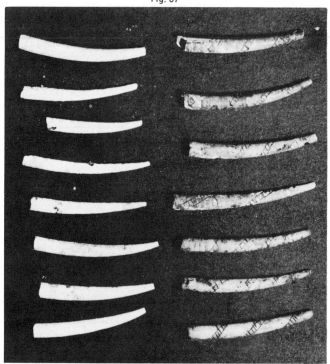

(Buehler collection)

DENTALIUM SHELLS
Those on the right are carved.

attaching more poles to the end of the first when the
water was deep. The thrust raised the board, allowing the
splints to spread; when withdrawn the weighted board
compressed the splints and entrapped any shells present
and the contrivance was then permitted to float to the
surface. The operation was repeated over and over, the
shells grew in beds and many a barren cast was made
before a bed was found. A dozen shells might be a day's

work. They were cleaned of their contents and then polished in a bowl of sand, although very little polishing was necessary. They are quite attractive, being clean, creamy white, and pleasingly formed. They grow in the sand, small end up; from this open end the animal within spreads tenacles to draw its food from the water.

All early writers mention this shell. Alexander Henry says, "We had an instance of the great value these people set on their sea shells. Mr. McDougall, having accidentally broken one belonging to his beau-pere Concomly, paid him 40 grains of large China beads, which did not seem to please the chief. The best quality are two inches long. One fathom of these shells is valued at three blankets of 2½ points. They are gathered northward, somewhere about Woody Point, N. of Nootka, in the sand, at low water." Ross says, "the circulating medium in use among these people is a small white shell called higua, about two inches long, of a convex form, and hollow in the heart, resembling in appearance the small end of a smoking pipe. The higua is thin, light, and durable, and may be found in all lengths, between three inches down to one-fourth of an inch, and increases or decreases in value according to the number required to make a fathom, by which measure they are invariably sold. Thirty to a fathom are held equal in value to three fathoms of forty, to four of fifty, and so on. So high is higua prized, that I have seen six of 2½ inches long refused for a new gun."

The dentalia were worn as necklaces, embroidery, head-dresses, and belts. A favorite method was to thrust one through the pierced septum of the nose. In modern times they were strung alternately with glass or copper beads when worn as a necklace.

Dentalia are found far into California and as far east as the Atlantic coast, showing the extent of the trade. Some of them were decorated with incised lines and patterns of delicate engraving, which must have increased the value considerably. The shells are still found in the sites of old burial vaults that were built on sand east of the Cascades. None are found in the moist climate of the West. They are no longer polished, having turned a chalky white, badly deteriorated, but still ornamental. Those now found are fairly modern, most of the prehistoric ones have disappeared long ago.

MISCELLANEOUS ARTIFACTS

A distorted perspective is apt to be formed of the furnishings of a typical Indian village because only the stone, and a few of the bone, articles are now found. Actually, stone implements were comparatively rare; bone or wood served to make nearly everything the natives used, espe-

Fig. 88

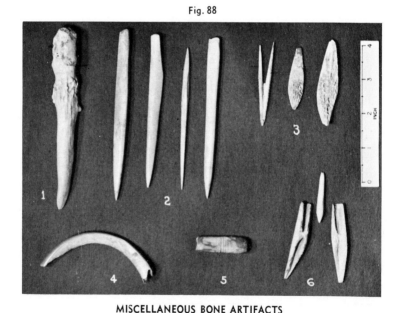

MISCELLANEOUS BONE ARTIFACTS

cially on the lower river. For every stone piece found, hundreds of wood and bone articles have long since decayed away.

The cedar was the most useful material the Western

Indians possessed. From it they could build and completely furnish their houses, including clothing, mats, baskets, eating and cooking implements, and weapons. Bone wedges felled and split the trees, bone and wood needles wove and formed the bark into useful products, beaver teeth and sharpened bone could be used to carve the wood into bowls and canoes. Stone was not essential for anything except cooking stones and sinkers. Arrows could be pointed with bone or fire-hardened wood, and frequently were. Gigs were made of wood with bone barbs. Even clubs and knives were made of wood and bone.

Prehistoric wood articles are no longer found along the Columbia, except where they have been constantly immersed in water, as in the drowned village site, MU 11, on Sauvies Island, or occasionally in a dry cave east of the Cascades. Bone implements are more plentiful, and the most common are needles and awls. These occur in many shapes, sizes and degrees of workmanship. Many are merely bone splinters ground to a point. Some are beautifully shaped and polished, and are sometimes decorated.

In Fig. 88 are a few representative bone artifacts. No. 1 is a flaking tool used for pressure flaking of stone tools and is made of a buck spike. Awls made of deer bones are shown in No. 2. No. 3 are natural fish or animal bones that are found in considerable quantities on the lower river but so far have defied identification, although examined by scientists of a large university. The one at the left is mistaken by many for a bone arrow point. Those on the right are frequently worked for some unknown reason; the center piece has been ground all around and has several incised lines on the polished back side. No. 4 is a beaver tooth, used for detail working on wood. Beaver teeth have extremely hard enamel which takes a very sharp edge. No. 5 is a section of bird bone, decorated; it may have been used for a bead but is more likely a gaming piece. No. 6 is the three-part fish spear found all along the river. The two collars are bound together around the point and to a cord about 12 inches long, which is attached to a shaft, as explained previously.

In Fig. 89 are shown some unusual bone tools found along the river. Their use is unknown but they may have been either an ornament for the hair or served some purpose in weaving. Some are two inches long, others three

Fig. 89

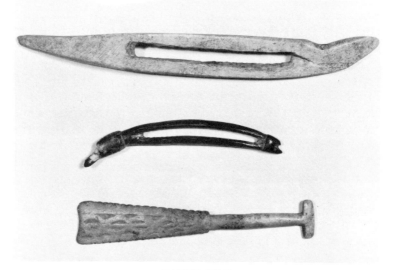

CARVED BONE

or four, and the long one illustrated is six inches. The shorter one is beautifully carved and polished, with an animal head on one end. It washed out of the bottom layers of the Shoto Village, CL 6, on Lake River. The canoe paddle is made of elk horn and is an exact replica of a common form of paddle used on the river. This one is highly polished but shows no marks of having been worn as an ornament. It is four inches long and also came from the Shoto Village.

The carved bone pieces in Fig. 90, are gaming bones found in Wakemap Mound by Carrel Morton. The one on the left had been inset with small discs of mica. Gaming bones are found all along the river and the bone game is centuries old; it is still played on the reservations in the same way. While in the village at the head of the Long Narrows near Wakemap Mound, attempting to trade for horses for their return trip across the continent in 1806, Lt. Clark observed and described this game (and a bit of human nature): "about 10 A.M. the Indians came down from the Eneeshur Villages (Celilo Falls, north side) and I expected would take the articles which they had laid by yesterday. but to my astonishment not one would make the exchange today. two other parcels of goods were laid by, and the horses promised at 2 P.M. I payed but little attention to this bargain, however suffered the bundles to lye. I dressed the sores of the principal chief gave some small things to his children and promised the chief some medicine for to cure his sores.

Fig. 90

BONE GAMING PIECES

His wife who I found to be a sulky Bitch and was somewhat afflicted with pains in heer back. this I thought a good oppertunity to get her on our side giveing her something for her back. I rubed a little camphere on her temples and back, and applyed worm flannel to her back which she thought had nearly restored her to her former feelings. this I thought a favorable time to trade with the chief who had more horses than all the nation besides. I accordingly made him an offer which he excepted and sold me two horses. Great numbers of Indians from defferent derections visited me at this place today. none of them appeared willing to part with their horses, but told me that several were comeing from the plains this evenging, among other nations who visit this place for the purpose of trade is the Skad-datt's (Yakima and Klickitat) those people bartered the Skillutes to play at a singular kind of game. in the course of the day the Skillutes won all their beeds skins arrows &c. This game was composed of 9 men on a side. they set down opposit to each other at the distance of about 10 feet. in front of each party a long pole was placed on which they struck with a small stick to the time of their songs. after the bets were made up which was nearly half an hour after they set down, two round bones was produced about the size of a mans little finger or something smaller and $2\frac{1}{4}$ inches in length. which they held in their hands changeing it from one hand to the other with great dexterity. 2 men on the same side performed this part, and when they had the bone in the hand they wished, they looked at their advorserys swinging arms around their shoulders for their advorsory to Guess which they performed by the motion the hand either to the right or left. if the opposit party guessed the hand of both of the men who had the bone, the bones were given to them. if neither the bones were retained and nothing counted. if they guessed one and not the other one bone was delivered up and the party possessing the other bone counted one, and for every time the advorsary miss-guessed untill they guessed the hand in which the bone was in. in this game each party has 5 sticks and one side wins all the sticks, once twice or thrice as the game may be set. I observed another game which those people also play and is played by 2 persons with 4 sticks about the size of a mans finger and about 7 inches in length. two of those sticks are black and the other 2 white and something larger than the black ones. those sticks they place in different positions which they perform under a kind of trencher made of bark round and about 15 inches in diameter. this is a very intricate game and I cannot sufficiently understand to describe it. the man who is in possession of the sticks &c. places them in different positions, and the opposit party tels the position of the black sticks by a motion of either or both of his hands &c. this game is counted in the same way as the one beforehand. All their games are accompanied with songs and time."

Another popular gambling game, played exclusively by

Fig. 91

CARVED SLATE

the women, used dice made of beaver or other animal teeth, or of bone. The markings varied, but essentially consisted of dots on one side and incised lines or plain on the other. Alexander Ross describes this game: "The women have also their own amusements. Their chief game, called omintook, is played by two only, with four beaver teeth, curiously marked and numbered on one side, which they throw like dice. The two women being seated on the ground face to face, like the men at chale-chal, one of them takes up the teeth, keeps shaking them in her hands for some time, then throws them down on the mat, counts the numbers uppermost, and repeating the sum thrice, hands the teeth over to the other party, who proceeds in like manner. The highest number wins. At this game trinkets of various descriptions and value are staked." In *Wishram Ethnography* the game is described somewhat differently. "The dice game was femenine; men never played it. It may have been played only in the winter and spring. The bone dice were four in number; seven inches long, a half inch wide, flat on one side, slightly convex on the other, somewhat pointed at the ends. These were marked in pairs on their convex faces, two called "men" had a line of crosses along the face, those called "women" had two longitudinal lines of dots, crossing which were transverse lines. Not all women had nicely marked dice. These were thrown from the hands. If two of a kind fell face up the thrower won a point; with any other throw the dice passed to an opponent." The beaver teeth dice are found all along the river but I have never seen any of the long bones described above. It is possible that some of the bone pieces shown in Fig. 90 are dice.

In the old village sites stone balls are found, varying from two inches to four or five in diameter, it is believed that they were used in some type of game. The balls are worked into near perfect spheres, but I have never seen one that was polished or decorated.

PART III
TRADE GOODS

THE LEWIS AND CLARK MEDALS

Trade articles have a special fascination—they form a concrete link between the present, the historic, and the prehistoric. The buttons and bangles picked up along the river are a symbol of a romantic past, when fur was king. For these baubles the natives traded their freedom and their heritage, as modern man exchanges his for a shiny car. Sir George Simpson complains: "Its returns this season are estimated at 2000 beaver got principally from a branch of the Nez Perces Tribe called Caiuses and it does not appear to me that there is a prospect of any considerable increase unless trappers are introduced as the Indians cannot be prevailed upon to exert themselves in hunting; they are independent of us requiring but few of our supplies and it is not until absolutely in need of an essential article or an article of finery such as Guns & Beads that they will take the trouble of hunting." High pressure advertising was lacking in those days, the Cayuses were not sold on the advantages of the white man's wares, although they were but one of the few tribes not made slaves by the white man's greed.

Tracing the history of trade articles is a fascinating but frustrating endeavor, for most of them have few if any identifying characteristics. One glass bead or one brass button is pretty much like another. The literature is practically nonexistent; a search of button books will identify some, while most tokens are listed somewhere. But the great majority of articles cannot or have not been traced—except guns which are well catalogued and need not be discussed here.

205

THE PEACE MEDALS PRESENTED TO PROMINENT CHIEFS
BY LEWIS AND CLARK

Fig. 92

Probably the rarest and most historic of all trade articles found along the Columbia are the Lewis and Clark medals. These medals are not strictly trade items for they were given to prominent Indians as a token of peace and friendship. Following a custom established by the home governments of the first colonies, the United States, soon after it was established, struck medals for the purpose of giving them to friendly Indians. The first one bears the date 1789, the year Washington was inaugurated as the first president. Similar ones followed, bearing the dates 1792, 1793, and 1795, and each succeeding president, except William Harrison, had medals struck bearing his likeness up to and including President Benjamin Harrison. Medals were very much prized by the recipients and many were handed down to their descendents, some were buried with their owners.

The medals carried by Lewis and Clark were of two types, the Jefferson Medal, and one called the "Washington Season Medal," bearing the date 1796 but not distributed until 1798, one year after the close of Washington's last term. This latter medal is silver, 1.75 inches in diameter, with a loop for suspension. The reverse has an inscription "Second Presidency of Geo. Washington MDCCXCVI" in five lines, surrounded by a wreath of oak and laurel. The obverse was made with three different designs, a woman at a spinning wheel, a farm scene, and a farmer sowing wheat; the latter was the one carried by Lewis and Clark.

The Jefferson medal was made in three sizes, 4.1, 3.0, and 2.2 inches in diameter. It was struck on two thin shells of silver fastened together by a collar, to which was attached a ring for suspension. On the obverse is a likeness of President Jefferson with the legend "Th. Jefferson President of the U.S. A.D. 1801." On the reverse are clasped hands, a tomahawk and peace pipe or calumet, and the inscription "Peace and Friendship." Several of the fur companies, including Astor's, made medals with a similar reverse, but with a likeness of a company official on the obverse.

A total of 23, possibly 24, medals were issued along the Columbia by Lewis and Clark. Of these one was listed as large, 16 small, one of the smallest size, and five where no size was given. On their downriver trip they gave a small medal to Yel-lep-pit, a prominent Walla Walla chief, with the promise of a large one on their return trip, and since they stayed overnight with this chief on their return it is highly likely that they fulfilled their obligation, although they do not specifically say so in their *Journals*. The historian George W. Fuller says that Yel-lep-pit displayed a Jefferson medal to David Thompson, Northwest Company explorer, in 1811.

Seven medals, or eight if two were given to Yel-lep-pit, were given out near the mouth of the Snake River, two near Alderdale, four in the vicinity of the Long Narrows, eight near the mouth of the Columbia, one at Ridgefield, Washington, and one at the Cascades. On March 26, 1806, the *Journals* state: "We gave a medal of small size to a man by the name of Wal-lal-le, a principal man among the Cathlamets, he appeared very thankfull for the honor conferred on him and presented us a large sturgeon." Another was given to Shar-har-war-cap, a Cathlamet chief. These may be the two Washington Season medals on display at the Maryhill Museum (in 1959) in the heirloom collection of Mary Underwood Lane, direct descendant of Chief Chenowith who was hanged in 1856 for participation in the Cascades Massacre. Chenowith's Indian name was We-la-wa.

In the 1890's a large Jefferson medal was found in a grave on a small island, possibly Goat Island, near Wallula; this may have been the large one given to Chief Yel-lep-pit as this was near his village. It is now in possession of the Oregon Historical Society. In *The Northwest Coast* James Swan says that William Tufts, supercargo of a trading vessel in the Columbia in 1807, secured one of the Washington Season medals from the Indians at the mouth of the river, and shows an illustration of it in his book, printed in 1857. It has been reported that another small medal was found many years ago at Fort Clatsop, making five in all that have been recovered. There are at least 18 of them yet to be found, unless some are in collections and not recognized for the valuable and historical souvenirs that they are. How many Jefferson and how many Washington Season medals were among those given out is unknown. The only record of the medals is a tabulation in *Articles Wanted by Capt. Lewis*, in the files of the Quartermaster Corps, U.S. Army. Under "Indian Presents" it lists "12 small medals—at War Office."

NORTH WEST COMPANY TOKENS

Second in historical interest to the Lewis and Clark medals are the North West Tokens, a brass coin 1.1 inches in diameter issued by the North West Company in 1820.

Fig. 93

NORTH WEST COMPANY TOKENS

This was one year before it merged with the Hudson's Bay Company. It was valued at one beaver skin. The North West Company came into existence in the winter of 1783-84 as a partnership organization, the partners to share in proportion to the capital invested. Such bitter rivalry sprang up between this new company, efficiently organized and managed, and the British chartered Hudson's Bay Company, that the future of the fur trade was threatened by the demoralization of the natives because of the intense competition. The NorthWest Company sent out various exploring expeditions. The most notable of these explorers was David Thompson, who opened up vast new territories. In 1813 the company bought Fort Astor and renamed it Fort George. Finally, at the urging of the British government whose taxes were effected by the ruinous rivalry, the two companies merged in 1821 under the name of the Hudson's Bay Company.

The American Numismatic Society states that the North West Token is quite rare and worth about $50. It is listed in Raymond's "The Coins and Tokens of Canade," and Breton's "Illustrated History of Coins and Tokens of Canada" (1894). The latter reference says only five were in existence when the book was published, one of which was in the collection of the Ottowa government. Since then several have been found along the Columbia; I can find no reference of any being found elsewhere in the West or in the East. A dozen were found several years ago in a cache on the Cowlitz River, near its junction with the Columbia. In the Maryhill Museum there are 14 in the heirloom collection of Mrs. Mary Underwood Lane, all in excellent condition. Don Gallagher of Cascade Locks has five, found on Sullivan Island near the Cascades. Frank Johnson of White Salmon, Frank Wilke of Bingen, Lloyd McLeod of The Dalles, Frank Buehler and Keith Will of Portland, Ernest Cowles of Grandview, and I each have one or two. A count of all of those known, with a reasonable allowance for those not reported, indicates a total of about 50 have been recovered on the Columbia. As far as is known, all were found at the mouth of the Cowlitz, Sullivan Island and the Cascades, and Upper and Lower Memaloose Islands. When I obtained my first one I called a coin dealer and asked about their history and value; of the history, he knew nothing, but said they were worth about three dollars. Some time later, wishing to get one for a friend, I called several coin dealers in the West and learned that none of the tokens were available, most of them admitting that they had never had or seen one for sale.

BUTTONS

Buttons are found along the Columbia in an almost endless variety of shapes, sizes, and materials. The great majority of them must remain forever untraced and without fame, their identity lost forever in the recordless past. They were, and still are, made by the millions, and there is no more reason to hall mark a button than a bobby pin. But a few, especially military buttons, have marks on the backs and ardent button collectors have traced out their history.

Before 1800 buttons were made entirely by hand and bear unmistakable evidence in the variety and imperfections in the designs. Late in the 18th century a mechanical engraver was invented, the buttons were chucked in a lathe and engraved with spiral or zig-zag lines, mostly on buttons with cast bodies too fragile for the punch embossing process. After 1800 the machine-made button made its appearance and was used in conjunction with the hand methods until about 1850, after which nearly all were machine made.. Coined designs, which were stamped with a single stroke of a die as coins are made, were little used prior to 1830 except for uniform buttons which could be made only by this process because of the bold and deeply embossed design.

Buttons have been divided into classes by collectors. The earliest was the link type which looked like a modern cuff link. The wedge type, not much used after 1800, had a cast or hand-wrought body; the shank was a wedge shaped projection that was drilled after the body was formed. This type was not popular as the shank was soft and wore through quickly, seldom lasting over a suit or two. Buttons were expensive and expected to last a while.

The Tombac or "T" type was cast around a wire loop which formed the shank. They were then put in a lathe and turned smooth. Tombac buttons were used but little after 1800, but are found in considerable quantities along the river. They can be identified by the smooth, turned body and the rough casting around the wire loop. The Alpha or "A" type has hand-wrought or cast bodies, the shank is made of hand drawn wire, often half round in the cross section, bent into a partial loop and brazed to the body. The small area in contact with the body made an insecure shank and this type was superseded by the Omega or "O" type about 1800. The loop on this button was bent at right angles where it made contact with the body, providing more area for a secure brazing. The Sanders or "S" type was invented early in the 18th century, it is made of two thin shells crimped together.

Most of the buttons were made of brass or bronze, but the composition varied widely since scrap was used extensively in compounding the metal. Copper was expensive and was not often used except when intended to be silver plated. All of the yellow metal buttons were plated, gilded, lacquered, or given some kind of coating. A special brass called tombac or white copper was made by adding arsenic to the copper and zinc, this metal has a silvery color. Many of the buttons from the river are of tombac.

Of the buttons bearing the manufacturers name on the back by far the most bear the name Scovill. Organized in 1802, the Scovill firm made a variety of buttons and other goods. It is now one of the largest firms in the United States. The date of a Scovill button can be estimated from the form of the name, as follows:

Scovill ....Before 1827
JHL & WH Scovill...............1827-1840
Scovills & Co......................1840-1850
Scovill Mg. Co....................1850
Scovill Mfg. Co....................1850 to present

Another prominent American button manufacturer was Aaron Benedict, who started making pewter buttons in 1812, later making the familiar yellow metal buttons. In 1829 the firm became Benedict & Co., in 1834 Benedict and Burnham, and in 1849 the Waterbury Button Company. About 1834 they commenced stamping "Treble Plate," "Double Gilt," "Extra Fine," and "Superfine" on the back of their buttons.

Fig. 94

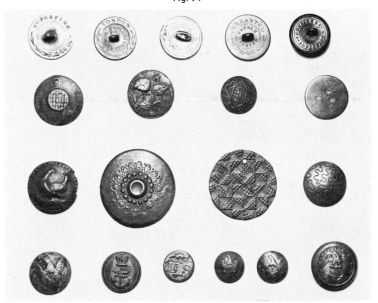

TRADE BUTTONS FROM THE COLUMBIA RIVER

Military buttons have been well catalogued and can be traced. Johnson's "Uniform Buttons, American Armed Forces, 1784-1948," covers hundreds of them. English military buttons are also well catalogued. They, as well as American, are found in many styles on the Columbia.

In Fig. 94 are shown some buttons found along the river. The top row shows some of the markings that are stamped on the backs. The bottom row is military buttons dating, left to right, after 1850; British, date not known; 1820; after 1840; 1840-1850; 1840-1850. In the second row, left, is a game or sportsman's button very popular in the early 1800's. The second button from the left in the third row has a cast design, the one on the right has an engraved design.

A dated button does not date a site. Old or out of date uniform coats were often used for trade, the Indians were very fond of them especially if highly colored, and they may have been quite old when traded. The fact that relatively few buttons have holes in them for a suspension cord proves that most of them were worn on clothing and not as bangles. Lewis and Clark tell of seeing natives on the river wearing uniform coats with large brass buttons. Metal buttons will last for years; there is no way of telling when they were brought into a site. Like all trade goods, they are not good dating material.

PHOENIX BUTTONS

Third place in interesting and historical trade items must go to the famed Phoenix buttons, found along the Columbia in considerable numbers as far as the mouth of the John Day River; they are quite rare above. They are also found along the coast and the Klamath Falls country. Several have been found in California, some on old mission sites, and a few in other states. The center of their distribution, however, was the Columbia River.

The button is named for its design, a Phoenix bird surrounded by the motto "Je Renais De Mes Cendres"— I am born again from my ashes. The Phoenix is a legendary bird dating from the fith century B.C. Every 500 years it would come to Egypt and build a nest in the Temple of the Sun, to which it was sacred. Setting the nest afire and fanning the flames with its wings, the bird was consumed to ashes, from which is rose again with renewed life.

Considerable work has been done by various persons in an attempt to trace the history and origin of these buttons, and while authorities do not all agree on the details, it has been established that they were intended for or used as uniform buttons by Henri Christophe, the "Black King of Haiti." Christophe was a remarkable man, blessed with powers of leadership and capability. A former slave, he led his fellow Negroes in an uprising against the French colonists of Haiti, and when the Island was declared independent in 1807, became its first president In 1812 he was crowned king. Under his domineering rule the Island became prosperous, and he built roads and public works, including some ornate palaces for himself. Eventually the people revolted against his arrogant leadership and in 1820, rather than be captured, he ended his life in a citadel he had built on a high mountain. The Phoenix bird was on his coat of arms, his crown, and officers sword belt buckles. Christophe had 32 regiments of infantry, three of artillery, and three of cavalry. Each button bears a number which is a regiment number.

Mrs. Nellie Church, ardent button collector of Portland, and the late N. G. Seaman, author of *Indian Relics of the Pacific Northwest,* carried on an extensive correspondence with authorities in the East concerning the buttons and believed that they were brought to Oregon by Nathaniel Wyeth. Wyeth was an energetic and resourceful man. Leaving a prosperous business in Boston, he traveled overland with a small party in 1833, sending a ship around the Horn with a load of goods to meet him on the Columbia. He started with three wagons having beds built as boats for fording streams. The three vehicles contained "a variety of articles or 'goods,' so called, calculated for the Indian market, among which vermillion and other paints were not forgotten, glass beads, small looking glasses, and a number of tawdry trinkets, cheap knives, buttons, nails, hammers, and a deal of those articles on which young Indians of both sexes set high value, and white man little or none" as recorded by a member of the expedition. The buttons may have been the Phoenix.

Wyeth's ship was lost. But he returned to Boston and outfitted another, the *May Dacre,* and went back to Oregon in 1834. He built Fort Hall on the Snake River and Fort William on Sauvies Island. He intended to start a salmon packing industry on the Columbia, and the trade goods were for purchasing fish from the Indians as well, of course, as furs. His venture failed, but the largest number of Phoenix buttons are found at the favorite fishing spots within transportation distance of his headquarters on Sauvies Island—the Cowlitz River, the Cascades, Clackamas River, and Oregon City Falls.

Fig. 95

PHOENIX BUTTONS

It is known that the Hudson's Bay Company did not bring them; this was determined by Mrs. Church and Mr. Seaman. They were on the Columbia prior to 1835, as several were found on the Multnomah village site which was deserted and burned to the ground by then. The evidence indicates that they were brought here by Wyeth and that he obtained them in Haiti. Prior to coming to Oregon he was an ice merchant and sent shiploads to the West Indies where that useful commodity was in great demand; he could have easily obtained the buttons then as the Oregon expedition had been in his mind for some time. After his failure on the Columbia he returned to the ice trade and made a modest fortune. Whatever the origin of the buttons, they were definitely linked to King Christophe.

There are two types of Phoenix buttons, disc and ball shaped. The disc buttons are found in two sizes, the larger being 0.95 inches in diameter and the small 0.6 inches. There are four styles in the large size with matching styles in the small, called style 1, 2, 3 and 4, reading from left to right in Fig. 95. Style 1 is by far the most common and so must be an infantry button. Style 4 is obviously artillery, it occurs only in numbers 1 and 2, but the large size is found with three different types of birds, matching those in styles 1, 2 and 3. The button numbers run from 1 through 10, 14, 20, and 25 through 30. There are no numbers 11, 12, 13, 15 through 19, or 21 through 24 found on the Columbia. They occur in the following number and styles, as determined from various collections I have examined:

No.	Large Style No. 1	2	3	4	Small Style No. 1	2	3	4
1	★			★	★			★
2	★			★	★			
3			★		★			
4	★				★			
5	★				★			
6	★		★		★			
7	★		★		★		★	
8	★				★			
9	★				★			
10	★				★			
14	★				★			
20	★				★			
25	★		★		★			
26	★				★			
27	★	★	★		★		★	
28	★				★			
29		★				★	★	
30			★		★			

In the larger sizes, 27 and 28 seem to be the most numerous, and 14 in the small size. Number 3, both large and small, is the rarest; I know of only one large number 3 in any collection, but there may be more.

The ball type Phoenix button, rare on the Columbia, is 0.65 inches in diameter and 0.52 inches thick, made in the Sanders or two-piece form. The bird is style 3. The lettering is the same script as the disc button, and the "No" is made the same way, a large "N" and a very small "o". All are No. 1 or 2, and the figure is exactly the same size and shape as the figure on the disc buttons. The design is indented, not raised, and quite shallow. They are very well made, the joint between the two pieces can hardly be seen, and the shank is evenly formed and securely fastened. It is quite likely that these buttons were made for officer's uniforms. In a museum in Lafayette, Indiana, there is an elaborate uniform coat of the 1810-1812 period with 33, originally 34, of the ball type Phoenix buttons sewn on it. They are all No. 1, as are most of those found on the river. All ball type Phoenix buttons are stamped "Bushby-London" on the back, so it

Fig. 96

BALL TYPE PHOENIX BUTTONS

is reasonable to assume that all Phoenix buttons were made by this firm, since the lettering and the bird design are too similar to be a coincidence. It is, however, possible that the dies were made by the same concern and the buttons were the product of different ones, but this is unlikely. In any event, they were made in England shortly after 1800. A note from the Registry of Business Names in England states that they have no record of the Bushby firm.

The ball type buttons were made of copper, possibly they were silver plated. The disc type buttons were made of two materials, brass and bronze, and very good material it was for some are found in mint condition although buried for decades. Style 1 buttons all have borders, style 2 and 3 do not, and some style 4 have borders and some do not. In all, at least 45 different dies were used in making them. The dies were well made and sharp, although some buttons were struck off center, losing part of the border.

The largest quantity ever found at one time was a cache of 200, found near the mouth of the Cowlitz River by two boys, Ralph and Dale Jones, several years ago. In the same cache were 12 Northwest Tokens and 30 Colonial buttons, and a quantity of other trade goods. Evidence where they were found indicated that they were in a trapper's or trader's cabin, or an Indian hut, that had burned. In 1895, two boys fishing on the Clackamas River found a washed-out grave containing 40 Phoenix buttons and 25 Colonials. Howard Galbraith found 26 washed out of the bank on Sauvies Island near the bridge. Over a hundred came from Sullivan Island near Cascade Locks. It appears that the total quantity found along the river is considerably less than 1000. There must have been a great many brought to the river, since what is found is always only a small part of the original quantity of any trade goods.

COLONIAL BUTTONS

One type of large button, Fig. 97, is called the "Colonial"; the name refers to the period in which it was made rather than the place of manufacture. During the latter half of the 16th century there was a surge of patriotism when Americans as much as possible made their own buttons instead of importing them from England. But the Colonials were also made and worn abroad. The early ones were made of bell metal, copper, or gold and silver plate, and later of brass. They reached the largest size around 1750, sometimes being made one and three-quarters inches in diameter.

Fig. 97

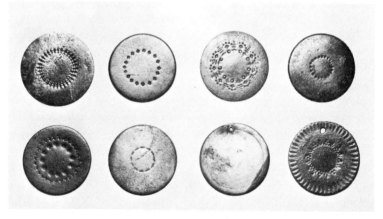

HAND MADE BUTTONS

They are beautiful buttons, no two of them are ever alike. They were made by hand. The design was imprinted by repeated application of a small punch with a round, square, diamond or other simple figured point, or by alternating with several punches with different points. As many as 150 strokes might be required to finish the design. The pattern is just irregular enough to be interesting, and serves to identify them. Instead of geometrical designs, some had flowing feather, flower or script patterns. The one second from the right in Fig. 97, has such a pattern but is so well worn that it did not photograph well.

Most of the buttons are round, from 1.2 to 1.5 inches in diameter, but a few were made octagon or oval shaped, and some were inlaid with mother of pearl. Few of the latter are found on the Columbia. Colonial buttons are found in the same places as Phoenix buttons, and frequently together. I once found eight Colonials and six Phoenix by scraping out the cracks in the bedrock with a knife blade on Lower Memaloose Island during low water. Several came from Sullivan Island. Very few are found above the John Day River. None ever have any markings on the back. The shank is made by bending the wire in a circle, and is brazed or soldered on.

GLASS BEADS

The first use of man-made glass was for beads. Archaeologists uncovered in Egypt some stone beads that were glazed with glass, made at least 5000 years ago and perhaps much earlier. About 3500 years ago the first translucent, purified glass was made—in the form of blue beads. Glass was then precious, like jewels, and saved for the nobility, but a few hundred years later glass became more common and small, white beads were made in large quantities. At the same time, in Syria, they were learning to make colored beads.

The Roman conquest ended the Egyptian glass industry, but the emperors imported skilled workers to Rome where the industry reached a high degree of art, and glass beads became so common that even the poor could wear them. By the year 1200 Venice was making glass and gradually rose to dominate the industry, keeping the workers virtual prisoners on the island of Murano to prevent the art from spreading. One of the most important products was glass beads for trade throughout the then-known world.

In the latter part of the 19th century, Bohemia dominated the bead industry; at one time there were 700 exporters located there. Made in untold millions, mostly in small plants, in many countries, in almost every conceivable size and shape, and for ages, it is no wonder that glass beads are so difficult to trace. There is no publication devoted to beads alone except for the work of Orchard. There are bits of information scattered throughout various periodicals and publications, but this is quite meager, for beads were so common that detailed description seemed unnecessary. And the various nomenclature used by the manufacturers, distributors, wholesalers, retailers and purchasers added to the confusion. For the information contained herein, I am indebted to Mr. Arthur Woodward, retired, of Altenada, California, formerly with the Los Angeles County Museum and the Museum of the American Indian. Mr. Woodward furnished me with a detailed report on trade goods and was very generous with his time and help. I also drew freely from Orchard's *Beads and Beadwork of the American Indian*, and various books and histories of the glass-making industry.

A glass tube was the starting place for the manufacture of most beads. An early method of making tubes was to attach an iron rod to one end of a pierced globule of viscid glass on the end of a blowing iron, the rod was then grasped by a boy who ran with it at full speed straight away to draw the tube out as far as possible before the glass became too cold. The tube was then cut up into sections. Globular beads were made by charging a drum with glass tubes of the proper size, along with a flux of charcoal and clay or other materials, to keep the beads from sticking together. The drum was then heated while rotating, and as the beads became soft they assumed a globular form. Barrel-shaped beads were made by catching a thread of viscid glass onto a rotating iron bar having a diameter corresponding to the perforation. The revolving bar drew out the glass thread and the operator mani-

pulated it until the desired size and shape was obtained.
There were, of course, many other methods of bead manufacture and constant improvement of the technique.

Glass beads were the earliest trade goods on the continent and have been the most popular ever since. Colum-
bus on his landing on Watling Island in 1492, gave the
natives strings of beads. A glass factory was erected in
Jamestown, Virginia, in 1622, and may have made trade
beads, although there is no evidence that it did. Lewis
and Clark had a large quantity, but had spent most of
them by the time they started back; shortage of this medium of exchange was one of their main concerns on their
return trip.

Beads are found on the Columbia in an almost unlim
ited assortment of sizes, colors, and shapes; most of them
can be duplicated in any dime store, but there are some
that have a great deal of historical interest. One of these
is called the star or chevron bead, called by the makers
"paternoster" or "Our Father" bead, Fig. 98, one of the
oldest and most expensive types. This type varies in size

Fig. 98

"CHEVRON" BEAD

from small up to one and a half inches long. Star beads
are usually formed of successive layers of glass, externally
a dark blue, then bright red, then pale green, each layer
separated by opaque white. The layers are worked into
a design so that when viewed from the end they look like
gear wheels, always with twelve teeth. These beads are

found throughout North America and parts of Europe and Africa. Some were found in Hawikuh, New Mexico, during excavation of that ruin, and were presumably brought in by the Spaniards shortly after 1500. Star beads were made in Murano, Venice, as far back as records go. In other areas they are usually found in 16th and 17th century sites; the only ones I have seen from the Columbia were found at Five Mile Locks on the Long Narrows.

Second in historical interest is one known to the trade

Fig. 99

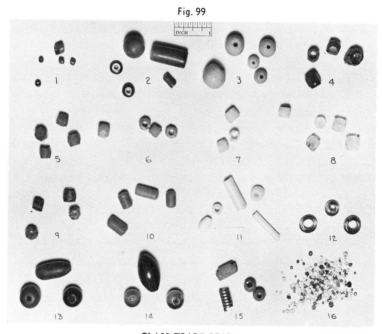

GLASS TRADE BEADS

as "Cornaline d'Aleppo" and commonly called Hudson's Bay beads. They are short tubular or oblate spheroid, and in length vary from one-eighth to one-quarter inch. Two colors of glass were used, the outer shell is a brick red, opaque, smooth, and shiny. The inner shell looks black but when held up to the light is a translucent green, an infallible test for this type. They are widely distributed in North America and the old world, and were made in Venice in the 17th and 18th centuries. They were a favorite with the Indians trading at the Hudson's Bay posts and some independent traders contributed to their distribution. While not common, they are found all along the Columbia. They are shown in Fig. 99, No. 1.

A later variety of the Cornaline d'Aleppo, Fig. 99, No. 2, is made with a semi-transparent red outer shell, and with a white or yellow core showing plainly at the ends. These occur in several tubular, ovate, and spherical shapes, the tubular ones may be an inch or more in length and the spherical ones a half-inch in diameter. The smaller ones are very fragile and break easily when handled, collectors when stringing them are dismayed to see them fall in half. They occur in large numbers along the river, especially in the later sites, and seem to have been confined to the northwest trade.

Another old bead found along the river is a large, translucent blue faceted variety with a large perforation, No. 4 in Fig. 99. They are found in the oldest sites and are more plentiful near the coast than on the upper river, indicating trading vessels as their source. Sometimes this is the only type bead found in a site, but copper beads seem always to be with them. They occur all along the Northwest coast and are generally called Russian beads, as they are the type used in the Alaskan trade, but they were not made by the Russians.

When Lewis and Clark were outfitting for their expedition they ordered "1. Blue Beads. This is a course cheap bead imported from China, & costing in England 15d the lbs. in strands. It is far more valued than the white beads of the same manufacture and answers the purpose of money, being counted by the fathom. 2. Common brass buttons more valued than anything except beads. 3. Knives, with fixed handles stained red, usually called red handled knives & such as are used by the N.W. Co. in their Indian trade". It seems that the useful knife took third place in the order of value. William Orchard believes these blue beads were the large faceted variety, they were called "Chief Beads" by the natives. At Fort Clatsop a visiting Indian "dressed in three very eligant Sea Otter skins which we much wanted; for these we offered him many articles but he would not dispose of them for any other consideration but blue beads, of these we had only six fathoms left, which being 4 less than his price for each skin he would not exchange nor would a knife or an equivalent in beads of any other color answer his purposes, these coarse blue beads are their favorite merchandise, and are called by them tia Commashuck or Chief Beads," wrote Lewis and Clark.

"Tyee comasuk" means in the Chinook jargon the chief of the beads or the best or superior, and does not mean that they were for chiefs only. James Swan says, "The women are fond of blue cut glass beads, which are highly prized. Light blue beads are worn only by slaves." Swan was on the Columbia nearly 50 years after Lewis and Clark and whether he was referring to the "Chief" beads cannot be determined, one of the other faceted varieties may have been fashionable by then. Light blue beads are found in large quantities and must have been very popular.

The most plentiful type of bead above the Cascades of the Columbia is a round, opaque, robins-egg blue variety having the appearance of glazed porcelain although they are glass, No. 3 in Fig. 99. They are found in at least five different sizes and seem to have been called Canton or China beads by the traders. Alexander Henry in his *Journal* says, "Sunday Apr. 3d. I now desired smelt to be traded at one fathom of small blue Canton beads for five fathom of smelt; yesterday we had traded at four fathoms". Also "Nov. 19th. Large blue China beads seem to be the principal article in demand". In the list of trade goods lost to the Indians during their attack on Stuart's party at the Cascades he lists "10½ lbs. Canton beads 2nd size. 10¾ lbs. Canton beads 3d size".

This bead Mr. Woodward believes to be the variety

known as the Chief beads. He says he has never encountered a statement that says they were manufactured in China. There were several British firms in China during the 18th and 19th centuries importing and exporting a variety of articles, and it is likely they were imported from Italy and redistributed. He says he has seen beads made in China during the 19th century, and they have a different appearance from those of European glass houses.

There were several types of faceted beads besides the blue Russian beads, some are shown in Fig. 99, Nos. 5 to 9. Faceted beads are made of hexagonal tubing, the facets were made with a spatula while the glass was plastic, or more rarely cut and polished by hand. The facets are generally crude and uneven, and the beads were broken from the tube leaving the ends rough. These beads are found in sites dating back to about 1830 and as late as 1870, they were very popular and widely distributed.

Another type of faceted bead was made of brass or other metal, about 1/16 inch in diameter. Since they are so small that they would be overlooked, their distribution is unknown. The only ones I have seen were in a string about six inches long that washed out of the bank near Cascade Locks, the copper salts had preserved the cord. They were made during the 19th century.

The smallest glass beads are less than one thirty-second inch in diameter, with a hole so tiny one wonders how they were threaded. They are part of a group called "seed beads"; the smallest are known to the trade as "Tinised" beads. They were used in making the famous decorated bags, ornaments, and clothing manufactured by the Indians throughout the Americas. Some of the creations involved an unbelievable amount of work. A Comanche cradle in the Museum of the American Indian has 120,-000 beads sewn on it, and every bead is threaded twice! Seed beads were made for a great many years but few are recovered because of their small size. They are shown in Fig. 99, No. 16.

The more modern beads are shown in Fig. 99, Nos. 10 to 15. White ones similar to No. 11 were made during the 18th century and are as old as the Chief beads. Large blue and green glass beads, like No. 13 and 14, were made

Fig. 100

POLYCHROME BEADS

as far back as the 17th century, but those found along the river appear to be modern. The light hollow copper beads shown in No. 15 are quite common along the river. The brass one is m a c h i n e wound and quite modern.

The polychrome or inlaid beads shown in Fig. 100, are by far the most beautiful and also were the most expensive. They are found in a great many patterns and colors, as they were made in Venice by families in their homes and not in factories; consequently, the fancy and imagination of the maker had full play. They may be inlaid, painted, gilded, spun, or made of varicolored glass. The fourth from the left in Fig. 100 is inlaid, made by fusing on strips of different colored glass to form flowers or patterns, much as the familiar glass blower at county fairs makes his baubles. Some are composed of glass threads spiraled around the perforation, these are called wire laid beads. Another type made with a grey-white background with round dots of red or blue encircled with a white ring, were called "Kitty Fisher Eyes", after the English actress of that name who died in 1767. Another was called "Pompadour", after the mistress of Louis XV of France. In the early 1800's glass tubing was shipped to

England for making fancy beads which were used as weights on lace bobbins.

The polychrome bead dates back to about 1800, although in the 1770's some were made and called "flower beads". Polychrome beads were very popular with the plains Indians, the greater quantities being found in the Crow and Blackfoot country. Most of those found on the Columbia come from the later sites, such as Upper and Lower Memaloose Islands. Frant Wilke has a string of them that were found while digging a basement near Bingen, Washington.

Wampum has become a common word designating shell beads, such as the small disc beads made of clam shells found in large numbers along the Columbia, Fig. 44. The genuine wampum, however, was a small cylindrical shell bead made of the quahog (Venus mercenaria) or hard clam, a very hard and brittle shell, although occasionally other shell was used. These appear in two colors, white and a varigated purple, the latter was the most valuable. Before the white invasion but few were made, because of the amount of work involved, and other shell and even stained wood was used. The whites, on learning the value of the bead, quickly devised methods of drilling and finishing them and Indians became customers instead of manufacturers, and large quantities appeared after 1650. Genuine wampum was made only in the East. It of course, varied in value. Roger Williams states that one fathom was worth five shillings, formerly nine. The usual size of the bead was about one quarter inch in length and an eighth in diameter, but some were larger. Prehistoric wampum was nearly always discoidal, but after the introduction of iron tools, making drilling comparatively easy, the tubular beads became the most popular. The genuine wampum is a beautiful bead.

The disc beads found along the Columbia should not be confused with the wampum of the history books. These disc beads were made by the Indians of clam shells, both fresh and salt water varieties. The shell was broken or cut into small pieces, then drilled. A number of drilled blanks were then impaled on a stick and pressed together, then with an abrasive stone dressed down to the desired diameter. They are found in quantity all along the river.

In the East the wampum served as money, in the West it was the dentalium.

COPPER ORNAMENTS

The earliest ornamental trade articles were copper bangles and rolled copper beads made by the natives from sheet copper. These are found in graves and cremations where no buttons or glass beads are found. Prior to 1800, Boston traders carried sheet copper on their ships. Captain Gray, discoverer of the Columbia, had 3495 pounds of copper aboard. Before copper, there were iron bracelets, but they were not strictly trade goods as they were made from nails taken from wrecked ships or driftwood. They can be identified by either a head or point on one end, or perhaps both. The rust is in flakes, identifying wrought iron. Some of the copper articles may be native copper from the Northwest coast, but a spectographic analysis is necessary to identify it as native copper. Rolled beads and bangles are made of sheet too uniform in size to be native, but occasionally a spherical bead or awl, or a small bangle, that might be native copper is found.

Mr. B. H. McLeod, consulting metallurgist of Stamford, Connecticut, examined some rolled copper beads found by Dr. Douglas Osborne in site 45-BN-3, near McNary Dam, and believes the technique used by the natives to make them was to hammer the sheet flat on the edge and more or less peen it out. Some round object was then used as an anvil, and the roll started by hammering the edge along the anvil; rolling was continued until the rolled edge touched the flat sheet. The anvil was not used after the initial upturning. Using the side of the bead as a guide, a knife was drawn back and forth along the flat sheet until a notch was started, then the sheet and bead

Fig. 101

COPPER BEADS AND BANGLES

bent back and forth until it broke off along the cut. The rought broken edge was then ground smooth and the cut end hammered to complete the tube. Rolled copper beads are found in large quantities along the river. The longest are six or seven inches, but most of them are one or two inches.

Copper bangles seem to be all of native manufacture. The holes are punched, then generally ground smooth. Their shape depended entirely on the whim of the maker, but occur in three general types, round, triangular, and rectangular, with the latter the most common. One favorite pattern was enlongated, straight-edged on the sides and top, narrowing toward the upper end, and about two times as long as broad. The bottom edge was cut with a saw tooth, V-shaped, semi-circular, or other simple design. Copper kettles, after their useful life was finished, often ended up by being cut into bangles. Copper to the Indians was as valuable as gold; indeed, it is as beautiful a metal when polished. Bangles were worn on a thong around the neck, as ear ornaments, or suspended from the clothing. The largest one I have seen measures 4 by 5 inches. Buttons and tokens, as well as coins, were frequently punched and worn as bangles, although of the 70 Phoenix buttons and 16 Colonials that I have, only three of each are disfigured with holes. North West Tokens always have holes for suspension since they had no hoops. A few bangles are decorated with punched holes or raised pattern marks, and occasionally one is hammered into a semi-globular or other odd form. Those cut into specific figures or designs are rare, two small ones are shown in Fig. 62.

TRADE AXES

The trade axe, commonly called a Hudson's Bay axe and known by them as an "eye dag," was made by the thousands by the blacksmiths at Fort Vancouver. Being perishable, few are found along the river anymore. A number in various stages of manufacture were uncovered at the site of Fort Vancouver, during excavations there under the direction of Louis Caywood; from them it is possible to determine the method of fabricating them. No whole ones were found, the Hudson's Bay Company was a very frugal organization and let no useful articles become carelessly lost.

To make an axe the blacksmith heated a bar of wrought iron about 15 inches long, and bent it around a mandrel that served as a form for the eye. The two ends were then brought together and drawn out to form the blade. A slot was left in the blade in which a thin sliver of steel was inserted. The whole was then blacksmith-welded into one piece and shaped with the hammer. The eye was then rounded out and finished; sometimes a short piece of bar was welded to the top to act as the head. All operations of course were carried out while the iron was hot. They were not handled. The Indians made their own from one of the many hardwoods found in the West; the vine maple was probably a favorite material.

Axes were made in widths corresponding to the bar sizes available, 2, 1¾, 1½ and 1¼ inches wide. They were a favorite and most useful trade article, and most likely the blacksmiths were never idle; when no other work was required there were always axes to be made. Some of the original Hudson's Bay axes are shown in Fig 102, the handled one at the bottom was still in use 50 years ago. The axe on the left is a pipe tomahawk,

Fig. 102

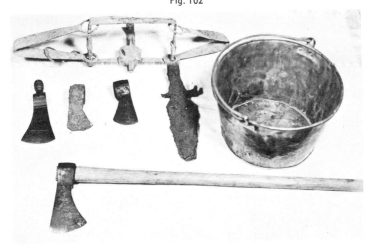

TRADE AXES, KETTLE, AND BEAVER TRAP

which was once common on the plains, but a few made their way to the far West. The next two are typical eye dags. The fourth is a blacksmith-made tomahawk, popular in the Columbia River area and used as a weapon only. Some of them were factory made of brass in England. A tomahawk of this type in the Oregon Historical Society museum has been identified as the one used to slay the Whitmans in the Whitman Massacre of 1847. At the top is an old Hudson's Bay beaver trap, and on the right is a typical brass trade kettle. All are from the extensive collection of Ernest Cowles, of Grandview, Washington.

MISCELLANEOUS TRADE ARTICLES

In Fig. 103, are shown some miscellaneous trade goods. No. 1 is a bracelet made from a wrought iron nail. It was found in a cremation pit dating back to shortly before 1800. In this large pit there were no glass beads whatever, but there were a few copper beads and bangles. Iron bracelets were also found in the Atlatl Valley site, known to be prehistoric. These nails were extracted from vessels that were wrecked on the rugged Oregon Coast, or from driftwood washed up on the beach. The natives were familiar with metals prior to the coming of the white man because of these wrecks; this prior knowledge was of great benefit to the first traders, as they received enormous prices for a bit of sharpened strap iron. The *Columbia* had 6,755 pounds of "Chissells" aboard. These old ship nails can be identified by either a head or point on one end, or sometimes both the head and point. The one in the picture shows the point only, the other end is badly deteriorated, probably because of the deformation from the efforts to cut it off.

No. 2 is a machine-made bracelet, a quite rare trade item dating back probably to 1850 or earlier. The material has been passed through rollers that imprinted continuous lines along the edges, then the design was made by repeated application of punches with different shaped points, much as the Colonial buttons were made. No. 3 is a bracelet made from a piece of copper wire bent to shape. This is the most common form. No. 4 is a pipe made from cast pewter, and was made to be used with a wooden stem. Evidently they were not very popular as few of them are found. In No. 5 are shown some of the various types of bells. The better ones are cast of brass, the cheaper ones of stamped metal. They were used as decorations on clothing and horses, and worn on the ankles to keep time while dancing.

No. 6 are brass finger rings sold by the thousands by the Hudson's Bay Company. No. 7 is part of a jews harp,

Fig. 103

MISCELLANEOUS TRADE GOODS

the steel tang has rusted away. This one is from the Hudson's Bay period, those from the American period have a much larger loop. Thimbles are shown in No. 8. They are found in considerable quantities and several sizes wherever trade goods appear. They always have a hole in the top, instead of using them for their normal purpose in sewing, the natives made little bells out of them to decorate their cradle boards, using beads for clappers; or they used them as bangles. Captain Gray carried in his cargo on the ship *Columbia* four gross of thimbles. No. 9 is a sideplate from a North West gun, which shot a round ball like those in No. 10. Diligent searchers of the shores of the Columbia find many of these round lead balls.

Nearly all of them turn out to be modern fishing line sinkers, but occasionally one of these interesting old relics turns up.

No. 11 is a hand-made nail. These can be distinguished from the modern machine-cut square nail by the slightly oval head showing marks of the blacksmith's hammer. They were made from bar iron by the early blacksmiths at times when there were no horses to shoe or other work to be done. No. 12 is a "chissell" of the type sold by the early traders. It was found on the surface at site 45-BN-3, as was the knife shown in No. 13, shortly before the Mc-

Fig. 104

DRAWER PULLS USED FOR BANGLES

Nary pool was filled. No. 14 are Chinese coins brought back by the fur traders when they sold their cargo in China. They were a favorite ornament. These coins were made into head dresses, belts, and sewn on native clothing. They are found all along the river.

Contrary to general belief, very few trade articles come from graves. The great majority come from old vault burial sites where all skeletal remains, being exposed above ground, has long since gone to dust. The rising waters and drifting sands continually expose areas, and the articles can be obtained by sifting. Some come from

cremation pits but are usually burned beyond recogni-
tion. Cremation fires were hot enough to melt copper
and glass.

Fig. 105

TOKENS

The objects shown in Fig. 104 have been identified by
Mr. Woodward as cast brass 19th century drawer-pulls,
and they were used for bangles by the Indians. One like
that on the left was found in the Multnomah village site,
so was brought to the river before 1835. Some of them
may have been taken from furniture discarded by the
pioneers on their way across the mountains when, due to
the loss of draft animals and the difficult roads, they had
to lighten their loads. And some, perhaps, may have been

taken from settlers' cabins after a raid. They are not plentiful on the river.

In Fig. 105 are shown two of the many types of tokens found on the Columbia. The upper one is the Log Cabin token used in the presidential campaign of William Henry Harrison. There were many of them made, and 26 varieties have been catalogued. The inscription reads "The Peoples Choice in the Year 1841", although some of them are dated 1840. The bank token is an example of the beautiful and elaborate designs used on some tokens.

The early fur traders carried a variety of items. The most popular were guns and ammunition, blankets, tobacco, and beads. In a cargo of goods going to the Spokane country in 1814 Alexander Henry lists five kinds of axes, awls, four kinds of blankets, steel tobacco boxes, horse balls, buttons, gun worms, gun flints, looking glasses, knives, darning needles, finger rings, six varieties of beads, six kinds of shirts, thimbles, steel and iron daggers, Canton thread, combs, gun balls, shot, gunpowder, brass and copper kettles, tea kettles, cod hooks, and tobacco.

The Columbia River was the center of activity and the main artery of commerce for the entire Oregon country. The first trader to enter the river was Captain Gray, in 1792. After that, ships regularly sailed into the bay across from Astoria to trade. The Chinooks readily acted as middlemen, trading the white man's goods up the river and up and down the coast for furs which they would hold until another ship arrived. Metal in any form was the most valuable trade item at first, but the shrewd Chinooks soon learned how eager the white man was for furs and began to strike harder bargains. They had their favorite traders, probably those who gave the most presents. They gave the names of the captains and described several ships to Lewis and Clark, while they were encamped at Fort Clatsop.

The first trading post on the Columbia was established

at Astoria in 1811 by the Pacific Fur Company, headed
by John Jacob Astor. It became the center of the distribution for the entire river; outposts were built at the mouth
of the Walla Walla, Okanogan, and Spokane Rivers. In
1825, Fort Vancouver was built by the Hudson's Bay
Company, and thereafter was the headquarters of the
company in the Oregon Country. Parties were sent all
over the country to trade for and to trap furs; there were
few beaver on the river itself but all the tributaries were
rich in them. The Columbia itself produced only the
salmon.

The value of trade goods of course fluctuated a great
deal. When there were rival traders in the vicinity the
natives benefitted greatly, for prices for furs went very
high, sometimes almost to their actual value. The Hudson's Bay Company dominated the Columbia trade because they could outbid any of the American traders,
knowing that any losses could be regained when the competition had been driven off.

From records at Fort McPherson on the Peel River in
Canada, Cornaline d'Aleppo beads sold at six for one
"made beaver;" a made beaver is one that is stretched and
dried ready for market and was the standard of value by
which all trade goods were sold. A light blue bead, ⅜
inch in diameter, was three for a beaver, and one ½ inch
was two for a beaver. A very large bead was worth two
skins. Seed beads sold in bunches of four or five strings
each four to six inches long, were worth one beaver each.
These prices were much higher than those on the Columbia when trade started there.

In his *Journal*, Sir George Simpson has a list "Standard
of Trade—Columbia River 1824-25," with the following
values at Fort George (Astoria) all in skins made beaver:
Axes, common—1; Blankets, 3 pt.—6; Blankets, 4 pt,
green—10; Beads, per lb.—1; Buttons, per doz.—1; Flints,
gun, per doz.—1; Guns, common N.W.—20; Rifles, English twist—40; Gun powder, per lb.—3; Knives—1; Kettles,

per lb.—2; Rings, brass, per doz.—⅓; Thimbles, per doz.—½; Vermillion, per lb.—4. These prices cannot be considered too bad. In return, the company paid ⅓ skin for a 30 lb. salmon, 1 skin for a gallon of berries, and 3 skins for a fresh elk. A good beaver skin was then worth three to five dollars at the market in China or England.

PART IV
ARCHAEOLOGICAL METHODS

DIGGING METHODS

The rapid destruction of archaeological sites by construction work, river dams, and erosion, makes it imperative that if digging is done, it be conducted in an orderly manner so that the scientific values may be preserved. Soon all the native sites will be gone; their record is important to complete the story of early man. It can be read only from the page on which it was written, the structure of the site itself; and if this page is destroyed it can never be reconstructed. If you must dig, do it properly. You will find it more enjoyable, because you are then doing something worthwhile. A collection completely catalogued and documented has not only a scientific value but an increased monetary value as well.

Fig. 106

E	1	2	3	4	5
D	1	2	3	4	5
C	1	2	3	4	5
B	1	2	3	4	5
A	1	2	3	4	5

ARCHAEOLOGICAL GRID

The first thing to do is to obtain the permission of the property owner to work a site. This is imperative. Federal and state lands are protected by antiquity laws and are excluded from amateur digging; serious amateurs are nearly always welcome, however, to assist the professionals, and that is the best way to learn the proper methods. After you have obtained permission from the owner, survey and map the site. Location can be by distance and direction from an established point, such as a town, or preferably a surveyed section corner. The map should show features such as river or stream banks, caves, and contours. Compass directions should be shown, the elevation of the area, and the ownership.

Next, photograph the site from all angles and choose some prominent location, usually the highest point, as a datum from which all measurements are to be taken. Mark off the area in a grid of five-foot squares, and drive a stake in each corner, marked with the square number. Draw the plan of the squares in the notebook, showing the "north" direction for orientation. The five-foot square is standard in the profession.

Fig. 106 shows a typical grid, the squares are designated by Row D Sq. 3 or Row B Sq. 6, etc. The grid gives what is known as horizontal control. From the marked artifacts, after excavation is complete, it is possible to tell exactly where each artifact came from, and association with each other can be established.

Vertical control is obtained by excavating in levels, referred to the previously established datum point. There are two kinds of levels, an arbitrary one such as six inches or a foot deep, and a geological one, which follows the natural stratification or structure of the site, the former is the most common. Vertical control is important because generally the objects found in the lower levels will be older, and when the site is reconstructed from the artifacts and data the cultural sequence of the inhabitants can be established. Sometimes an abrupt change in artifacts indicates a distinct cultural break, such as strong influence

from another tribe or outright capture. Such breaks are of
the utmost importance in tracing migrations. If all sites
were properly excavated and documented, and the information made available, a map could be drawn showing
the migrations and cultural changes.

Suppose a one-foot level is chosen for your excavation.
Obtain a supply of eight-pound paper sacks and mark one
with the number and level of the square on which you
are going to start. Begin at one corner of the square, being
careful not to disturb the stake, and excavate down one
foot, keeping the floor level, which means that all of the
first level may not be one foot deep but no part should be
more. Place all the artifacts from this level in the sack,
and be sure to save the broken ones, and all the game and
fish bones, which are important to show the food habits
and environment of the people, and the distribution of
animal life.

The sides and bottom of the trench must be kept
straight and clean, this can be done only with a square
point shovel. The flat bottom of the trench will reveal
features such as pits or fireplaces, which should be recorded in the notebook. When the excavation of the
square is complete, sketches should be made of the vertical walls showing the stratification and features. Important features should be photographed, those too faint to
show in the picture, such as floor levels, can be outlined
with short sticks or straws. It is not necessary or desire-
able to excavate each square completely before going on
to the next, rather the work should take the form of a
trench in a series of short steps.

If an important feature such as a fireplace or a burial is
encountered, it should be carefully excavated, removing
the surrounding soil with a trowel and brush so it can be
photographed. If it extends into the next square, then
that one should next be removed in the regular manner,
leaving the entire feature exposed. When photographing,
always use some familiar object such as a trowel or shovel
for a scale, or better yet use a ruler with figures large

enough to show in the picture, and a card showing the site, square number, and level. The best camera to use is one of the press type, with a ground glass for focusing, although any good camera will serve if it will focus down to three feet, and care is used in focusing. A tripod should always be used, and a light meter is helpful.

Some organic material, preferably charcoal but bone or any organic material will do, should be preserved from important sites for possible future "carbon 14" dating, it should be taken from the lowest levels or specific areas for which a date would be the most important. It must be taken from below the level of grass and tree roots which will give a false reading unless great labor is used to remove them. Place the material in a fruit jar with a tight fitting lid or wrap it tightly in plastic. Carbon dating is a very precise and expensive operation; few amateurs can hope to obtain one.

Fig. 107

CONTROLLED DIGGING BY AMATEURS, WAKEMAP MOUND
The area was blocked off into five foot squares, the material excavated to bedrock and screened into wheelbarrows.

Perishable material, such as bone or wood, will disintegrate after removal from the soil if not properly treated. The pieces should be wrapped loosely in waxed paper and put away to dry, then cleaned carefully with soft brushes.

The object should then be soaked in celluloid dissolved in acetone, gum arabic dissolved in water, or alvar dissolved in acetone—materials which can be obtained from a drug store. Some collectors use a solution of white shellac, one part, and alcohol, nine parts. This will be absorbed throughout the piece and after the alcohol evaporates the shellac will hold it together without altering the appearance. Never paint an object with shellac or varnish, it will change the looks completely. For the removal and preservation of fragile objects *in situ*, see some good textbook, such as *A Guide to Archaeological Field Methods*, by Robert F. Heizer, an excellent book for the serious student. The process is too involved to describe here.

All material should be marked with waterproof ink for identification. A code may be selected that will show the site, square, level, and artifact number — information which should be recorded in the catalog. Sites are numbered by the Smithsonian Institution system, using a code consisting of the number of the state when alphabetically listed, the county, and the site number. Thus 45-BN-3 would be the third site recorded in Benton County, Washington. Sites in Oregon would have the number 35. India ink is good for marking, using a crow-quill pen, followed by a light coat of shellac or fingernail polish over the number to preserve it. Put the number in an inconspicuous place and make it small but legible.

Excavations of caves is discouraged. These should be left intact for the professional, as a cave offers the most ideal conditions for preservation of archaeological evidence, and practically all caves are in places that are safe from destruction by the progress of civilization. New scientific investigation methods are continually being discovered; future archaeologists will have vastly improved facilities for dating and tracing.

Dating by the "carbon 14" method is the only precise method of establishing the age of a prehistoric site, except for the method of tracing growth rings, called dendrochronology, of trees used in house construction in the

Southwest. Carbon 14 is an isotope of carbon with an atomic weight of 14, instead of the normal 12, and is formed at a constant rate in the atmosphere by bombarding of nitrogen atoms by cosmic rays. All living things, both plants and animals, absorb carbon 14 in the same definite proportions. Upon death, absorption stops.

Carbon 14 breaks down at a precise and constant rate such that half of any amount changes in 5,568 years. Since no more carbon 14 is absorbed after death to replace that broken down, by taking a specimen and finding out how much carbon 14 is left in it, it is possible to date it very closely. Essentially, the process consists of purifying the sample and subjecting it to a form of geiger counter, the number of clicks is an indication of the amount of carbon 14 left in the sample. Fantastic precision and care are required, for the amount of carbon 14 is very small, and there is considerable background radiation that must be filtered out. There are methods of estimating age, such as geological formation, fluorine content of bones, and pollen analysis, but none are as precise as carbon 14 and dendrochronology. However, these two rapidly approach an age beyond which they are no longer useful.

Last but not least, a complete report should be written of the excavation, and this report submitted to the Department of Anthropology of your State University, or to the State Library or Museum, so it will be available for reference. The artifacts and other material should be kept intact for possible study by institutions or professional archaeologists. For the method of preparing a report, see one of the archaeological papers in the bibliography in the back of this book, or look at the magazine *American Antiquity* in the library. Such comprehensive reports are of course beyond the capabilities of the amateur, but a clear, concise, detailed report can be made by anyone, and is all that is required. Deductions should be left to others.

CODE OF ETHICS AND STATEMENT OF POLICY OF THE

WASHINGTON ARCHAEOLOGICAL SOCIETY

1. With the full realization that scientific and historical work in archaeology involves a complete recording of an excavation and its results, I pledge myself to do no digging on sites of known archaeological value until I am familiar with the fundamentals of archaeological technique. By archaeological technique it is meant that simple excavation by measured levels and the recording of artifacts and other finds by these levels is understood and followed. A profile sketch of any soil levels or changes and the records of the dig, but not necessarily the artifacts, are to be filed with the Society. The Society encourages individual and group exploration for new sites, by Society members and within the scope of the Code of Ethics.

2. I, realizing that the archaeological remains of our state are a finite resource, and one which is not only of purely scientific value but is of great popular interest and appeal, do pledge myself to make all reasonable effort to conserve and save archaeological deposits and manifestations for future generations. Where destruction is inescapable, as with erosion and construction, I shall devote myself to salvage, in terms of 1, above.

3. I pledge myself to work with and under the scientific direction of competent professional archaeologists on Society excavations. The Society's plan of procedure involves five steps and I pledge myself to follow them:

A. SURVEY
    1. To use professional methods and forms.
    2. To file, at the Washington State Museum, a complete record of sites together with photographs, tracings or drawings of artifacts found or photographed from local collections, together with pertinent observations.

3. To make available as loan or gift (on terms of mutual agreement) to the Washington State Museum any artifacts from surface collections that may be designated as type specimens.

B. EXCAVATION

1. To participate in Society excavations which shall involve digging according to established archaeological techniques.

2. To work under the control of Society officers by the Board of Directors and the President on Society excavations.

3. To place all records, artifacts and observations made while working on a Society-sponsored dig in the Washington State Museum or another designated museum as part of the permanent records. When, following the judgments of the archaeologist-in-charge and the officers of the Society, a sufficient sample of an archaeological deposit has been secured, the Society controlled dig may be terminated and further sections of the deposit may be worked on an individual basis as a contribution to a widened understanding of the site. Techniques used are to be those of the Society dig; artifacts recovered are to be catalogued properly but may remain in individual collections.

C. I further pledge that I shall devote myself to the preparation of records or reports that may be published in order that our work shall not be lost in files and on Museum shelves.

D. I pledge myself to work with State and County museums to aid in the care and conservation of collections and to aid in the preparations of displays which will bring to the general public an understanding and feeling for the prehistory of the area.

E. I pledge not to commercialize material which I collect and to discourage commercialization and faking of archaeological materials.

BIBLIOGRAPHY

BELDEN, B. L., "Indian Peace Medals", American Numismatic Society, 1927.

BOAS, FRANZ, "Primitive Art", Dover Publications, New York, 1955. Unabridged reprint of the first edition published in 1927. Profusely illustrated. A complete discussion of primitive art.

CAIN, H. THOMAS, "Petroglyphs of Central Washington", University of Washington Press, 1950. 54 pages. Describes the petroglyphs and pictographs on the upper Columbia from Vantage to the Okanogan.

COLLIER, HUDSON and FORD, "Archaeology of the Upper Columbia Region", University of Washington Press, 1942. Salvage operations in the Grand Coulee reservoir. 177 pages, 22 plates, maps.

COOK, S. F., "The Epidemic of 1830-1833 in California and Oregon," University of California Publications in American Archealogy and Ethnology, Volume 43, No. 3, Pages 303-326, 1955.

COX, ROSS, "The Columbia River", University of Oklahoma Press, 1957, a reprint of the edition of 1831. Cox was a member of the original Astor party.

CRESSMAN, DR. L. S., "Petroglyphs of Oregon", University of Oregon Publications in Anthropology, 1937. 78 pages, plates, maps. Does not discuss the petroglyphs on the Columbia but covers all others in Oregon.

DOUGLAS, FREDERICH H., and D'HARNENCOURT, RENE, "Indian Art of the United States", Museum of Modern Art, 1941. Plates of outstanding examples of primitive art.

FRANCHERE, GABRIEL, "Narrative of a Voyage to the Northwest Coast of America in the Years 1811, 1812, 1813, and 1814," New York, 1854. Franchere was a member of the original Astor party. His book is a classic and his descriptions of the natives on the Columbia are factual. Rare .

FULLER, GEORGE W., "A History of the Pacific Northwest", Alfred A. Knopf Co., 1945.

GASS, PATRICK, "Journal of the Voyages and Travels of a Corps of Discovery", 1811, reprint by A. C. McClurg & Co., 1904. Gass was a sergeant with the Lewis and Clark expedition.

GUNTHER, DR. ERNA, "Ethnobotany of Western Washington", University of Washington Press, 1945. All the plants that were used by the western Indians, and how they were used.

249

HASKIN, LESLIE L., "Wild Flowers of the Pacific Coast", Binfords and Mort, Portland, 1934. Flowering plants used by the Indians are identified.

HENRY, ALEXANDER, "Journal", edited by Elliott Coues, Frances P. Harper Co., 1897. Three volumes. 169 pages cover the Columbia. Henry arrived at Astoria in 1814. Rare, but one of the best.

HINES, REV. GUSTAVUS, "Exploring Expedition to Oregon", Geo. H. Derby and Co., Buffalo, 1851. First-hand account, with some good sightseeing.

JOHNSON, DAVID F., "Uniform Buttons, American Armed Forces, 1784-1948", two volumes, Watkins Glenn, New York.

KANE, PAUL, "Wanderings of an Artist Among the Indians of North America", 1858. The Radison Society of Canada, reprint, 1925.

LEWIS AND CLARK (see Thwaites).

OLSON, DONALD L., "Adze, Canoe and House Types of the Northwest Coast", University of Washington Press, 1927.

ORCHARD, WILLIAM C., "Beads and Beadwork of the American Indians", Museum of the American Indian, Heye Foundation, New York, 1929.

ORDWAY, JOHN, "Journal", State Historical Society of Wisconsin, edited by Milo M. Quaife, 1916. Ordway was a sergeant with the Lewis and Clark expedition. How the Columbia and its inhabitants looked to an uneducated soldier.

OSBORNE, DR. DOUGLAS, "Excavations in the McNary Reservoir Basin", Smithsonian Institution, Bureau of American Enthnology Bulletin 166, 1957. 257 pages, 40 plates, maps.

PARKER, REV. SAMUEL, "Journal of an Exploring Tour Beyond the Rocky Mountains", 1840. Rare.

RAY, VERNE F., "Lower Chinook Ethnographic Notes", University of Washington, 1938. 136 pages, 6 plates, map.

RELANDER, CLICK, "Drummers and Dreamers", Caxton Printers, 1956. Story of the last of the Wanapums who lived at Priest Rapids.

ROSS, ALEXANDER, "Adventures of the First Settlers on the Oregon or Columbia River", 1849. Reprint by Lakeside Classics, 1923. Ross was a member of the original Astor party.

ROSS, ALEXANDER, "The Fur Hunters of the Far West", 1855. Reprint by the University of Oklahoma Press, 1956.

SEAMAN, NORMA G., "Indian Relics of the Pacific Northwest", Binfords and Mort, Portland, 1946. The Indians of the Columbia River and Central Oregon and their artifacts.

SIMPSON, SIR GEORGE, "Fur Trade and Empire", Harvard University Press, 1931. Journal by Simpson, Governor of the Hudson's Bay Company, of his trip to the Columbia in 1824.

SPENCER, OMAR C., "The Story of Sauvies Island", Oregon Historical Society, 1947.

SPIER, LESLIE and SAPIR, EDWARD, "Wishram Ethnography", University of Washington, 1930. 132 pages, 13 plates, map. The Indians along the Long Narrows.

STALLARD, BRUCE, "Archeology in Washington", State of Washington, Department of Conservation, 1958. 64 pages, plates, drawings.

STRONG, SCHENCK, and STEWARD, "Archaeology of The Dalles-Deschutes Region", University of California Press, 1930. 182 pages, 28 plates, maps. One of the best reports on the mid-Columbia area. Scarce, out of print.

STRONG, THOMAS NELSON, "Cathlamet on the Columbia", Binfords and Mort, Portland, 1906. Told by a man who spent his boyhood at Cathlamet among the Indians.

STUART, ROBERT, "Journey of Discovery", University of Oklahoma Press. The journal of Robert Stuart, one of the original Astor party, of his journey from Astoria to St. Louis in 1812.

SWAN, JAMES G., "The Northwest Coast, or Three Years Residence in Washington Territory", Harper & Brothers, New York, 1857.

THWAITES, RUEBEN GOLD, "The Original Journals of Lewis and Clark", The Arthur F. Clark Co.,1905. The journal of this epic journey exactly as written, including all maps, and correspondence before and after the journey. Seven volumes and atlas. Rare and valuable. There are other editions but they are condensed, DeVoto's is one of the best.

TOWNSEND, JOHN K., "Narrative of a Journey Across the Rocky Mountains", 1839. Reprint, 1905, by the Arthur H. Clark Co. Townsend was a scientist with the Wyeth expedition.

WILKES, CHARLES, "Narrative of the United States Exploring Expedition During the Years 1838-1842", Philadelphia, 1845. Volumes 4 and 5 of five volumes cover the Columbia. Scarce.

WINEGART, PAUL S., "Prehistoric Stone Sculpture of the Pacific Northwest", Portland Art Museum, 1952. 58 pages, 42 plates, covering outstanding stone age work found along the Columbia and Fraser Rivers.

Periodicals: American Antiquity
American Anthropologist
Screenings, Oregon Archaeological Society

Unpublished Manuscripts: Caldwell, Warren, Ph.D. Thesis
Cressman, Dr. L. S., Report on Sites
WS 1 and WS 4

INDEX